—— Robert A. Clark ——

AF207983

Never Let 'em Quit

—— HOW ——
SCUBA INSTRUCTORS
CAN MAKE CONFIDENT,
LOYAL DIVERS OUT OF
any STUDENT.

IMPORTANT READER NOTICE

It is important that the readers of this book handle the information with care. It would be a mistake on the reader's part to assume that my observations and opinions about diving instruction are the final word on the subject. While my conclusions are based on sound logic and considerable experience, it is unlikely that what I have presented will apply to every situation. As such, the contents of this book should be considered in context and applied as the reader feels it is appropriate.

The intent of this book is to encourage a philosophy regarding the training of divers that will maximize their enjoyment and safety throughout their course of instruction. It is also intended to give the instructor a real-life understanding of what being a scuba instructor is all about without glossing over the downside. My hope is that the reader will embrace the spirit and intent of my efforts and grasp the essence of *how* to teach as opposed to *what* to teach. The *what* is being left to the certification agencies.

With the exception of those parts that are credited specifically to others, the contents of this book are strictly my opinions based on my personal experience as a scuba instructor and instructor trainer for more than 30 years.

© 1997 ▦ Concept Systems, Inc.

ISBN: 1-880229-41-2

First Edition
    First Printing, 4/97

PRINTED IN THE USA

Concept Systems, Inc.
2619 Canton Court • Fort Collins, CO 80525-4498 • (970) 482-0883

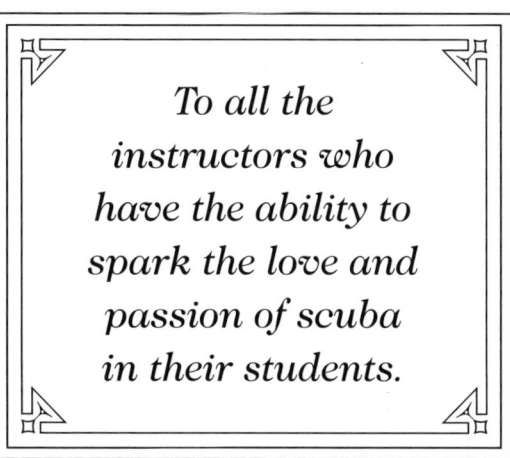

*To all the
instructors who
have the ability to
spark the love and
passion of scuba
in their students.*

Contents

Acknowledgements

There are several special people who I want to thank for their careful review of this book. They are individuals whose opinions I trust and who have, each in their own way, been of significant benefit to the diving industry. I am honored that they would donate their valuable time to keep tabs on an old friend.

Ed Christini, who has become my conscience. Dennis Graver, who has written many fine books of his own, and makes me pay attention to details. Jere Hallenbeck, a retailer who is not only successful, but also has the ability to get to the heart of the matter. Jon Hardy, an old friend and a recognized leader in diver education who, during our many projects together, has always offered me another valid point of view to help keep my mind open. Steve Linton, who has been like a younger brother for more than thirty years, and who is an expert on diving accidents. David Pratt, my computer guru, and without whose help this would never have gotten on paper. And last but not least, John Wall, another highly successful retailer who has proven to be a most valuable resource from the Dealer's perspective, and who has been more than generous with his time.

The two people I would like to thank most are no longer with me. Together they formed the foundation for my philosophy of life and set the standard for personal performance. They were the two finest human beings to have touched my life. The first was my grandfather A.S. Hardy, who taught me more about how to conduct my life and business than anyone or anything, including business school. The second, and most profound, was my father Robert Clark, Sr., who was more than a dad; he was also my friend. He took up where my grandfather left off and set in stone my ethics and social beliefs. I wish they were here—but they will always be with me.

Introduction

This book is quite a bit different from other texts. For one thing, the way it is written is designed to be more friendly. The problem with "textbooks" is that they're stuffy—almost like they were written in a very formal way just to impress you with how smart the author was. Well, we're not going to do that. This book is for real people who teach other real people how to dive. The whole idea is to make diving instruction easy and fun. It seems to me there is no reason a book about how to do that shouldn't be as easy to read and as interesting as it can be, even if it isn't quite fun.

Being a scuba instructor is a very special kind of teaching job. Not that it's hard. On the contrary, it is a real pleasure and one of the most interesting and challenging things you'll ever do. But, it is special because, unlike teaching in a formal school setting, you will be dealing with people of all ages and education levels, with widely varying reasons for being in the class, and huge gaps in abilities. If that sounds a little overwhelming, don't worry. What it is is a great challenge, and if you approach it with the right attitude, it will be highly enjoyable and extremely rewarding.

As a scuba instructor you're going to find that you need to wear several hats at the same time. You have to be a teacher, a psychologist, a disciplinarian, a diplomat, a travel agent, a salesman, and lots more besides. That's what this book is really about, how to be all of those things *when you need to be*, without even giving it a second thought. Oh yes, and that also includes being a mind-reader.

One thing that should be made clear right at the start is that the material required by the student to learn to dive is not a huge body of information. All of it is important, but experience has shown us the precise areas of information that are critical, and they have been systemized to the extent that what to teach is not really the problem. The problem is how to be a good teacher without falling into the trap of wanting to change and/or embellish the system, to avoid becoming bored with teaching the same thing over and over. The answer of course is simple: the challenge is not with what you teach, the challenge is the students themselves—especially those who need a little more help and understanding than the gifted students. Ask yourself this question: Who offers the greatest satisfaction to you as an instructor—the gifted student who instantly does everything perfectly, or the one who apparently can't do anything, but whom you eventually turn into a good diver? Not too tricky a question, is it?

This book is about the learning process. Why and how people learn. It is also about why people don't learn, which may be more important than why they do. It's about teaching people to be safe by training them not to get into trouble in the first place, but since there are always going to be a few people who will get into trouble anyway, it also covers the how's and why's of what to do if there is a problem. We call this contingency training.

Another big decision for every instructor is when to pass a student and when not to. There are lots of considerations either way, the most important of which is safety. I've included some solid objective criteria for helping you make some very subjective decisions about this critical area of concern. When it comes time to tell a student that they aren't ready to be certified, you don't have to automatically write them off as a lost cause and assume they are no longer a customer. I'm going to show you how to turn that person into one of your most loyal supporters.

Finally, the biggest downside to business in general is the liability concern. Of special interest to us are the legal aspects of teaching people to dive. Any rational person should know that when you enter an environment that won't support life without the use of special equipment, you entail a certain amount of risk, even to your life. I can't guarantee you won't ever have a problem, but this section can definitely help you understand how problems develop, and if one should, it can help you through it.

CHAPTER 1

The Learning Process

Let's start off with a little plain talk about the adventure we're about to undertake. I would guess that if you asked a few hundred educators about the learning process, you would most likely get a few hundred different answers. Everyone thinks they're an expert. So, I guess that makes me no different. It might even prompt you to ask why I would be so presumptuous as to think I know something more than they do (whoever "they" are). It would be a fair question even if you hadn't thought of it, so I'm going to give you the answer. I don't think I know more, but I have been teaching diving for over 30 years, and what I have to say here is nothing more than the result of my personal experience, combined with years of observation and research into why people learn, and why they don't. It is an effort to clear away all of the gobbledygook and offer some practical information to help you figure out how to teach people to dive in a more effective way. To help you help them find more joy in the process, and to put into perspective the fact that scuba diving is a fun thing to do. It should follow that learning how can also be fun, or at least it shouldn't be the least bit intimidating.

Since the early 1960s, I have personally trained several thousand scuba instructors, and many, many more divers. During that time I found that some people learned very fast, and some were quite slow. The interesting part was that the speed at which they learned was not a function of intelligence or even ability. It was either motivation, desire, or some unknown cause that I came to call a barrier to learning.

Times in the scuba business were hard in the '60s, and they aren't much different now. But at that time every student was critical to the financial success of my business. That meant that every student had to complete their course and become certified. No failures! Of course that goal might seem a bit unrealistic unless you planned to just rubber stamp everyone and certify them regardless of their abilities. But that was the goal. We never did make 100%, but we did real well.

I always knew that if students got their certification and weren't really comfortable in the water, they weren't going to buy any equipment. If they didn't buy anything, I couldn't buy groceries so the goal was not just to get everyone certified, but to make sure they were good. And not *just* good, but *so* good that they wanted to go diving more than anything. Because if they were good, and they wanted to go diving, they had to have equipment. It really is a simple formula: do a good job, train people to be capable, and you have great customers that buy your products. Everyone wins!

Easy to say, but not always so easy to do. In fact, setting the goal for every student to become a quality diver is probably unattainable. But not by much. The trick lies in you finding out why each person wants to learn to scuba dive, and how they learn. That is, what style of learning applies to them. Do they learn best with reward and punishment, or are they better readers or watchers or listeners? Every individual receives information differently, and is able to understand better from one source than another. Your job is to find out which source is the right one. Also, the motivation for taking the course is very important, because when you strip everything else away, people learn best when they have a clear "need to know." If a person doesn't believe that information is important to them in some obvious way, they will only process and retain for use, bits and pieces or none at all.

Another important piece to the puzzle is why people don't learn. What I call barriers to learning. As we go along, we're going to look carefully at most of the things that occur during a scuba course that can actually work to prevent people from learning the important skills that you are teaching.

Finally, the most important thing of all is making the people feel safe and comfortable in the water. This is a two-step process. The first step involves teaching people to dive in a way that prevents them from getting into trouble in the first place. I call these preventative skills, but what it really is is defensive diving. That is, diving in a manner that always assumes the worst can happen, and then staying within the safety parameters that ensure trouble won't follow. The second step is contingency training. This involves teaching people what to do if all else fails and they get into trouble in spite of their best efforts not to. The combination of these two factors is what makes a diver feel they can deal with whatever comes up. Of course this assumes that they become proficient in all of the skills involved. If they aren't good at them the whole concept collapses.

So to recap before we launch into the details of this fascinating journey, we are concerned with just three things: why people learn, why they don't, and making them safe and comfortable in the water. We have a lot of ground to cover to make the journey clear, but it should be easier knowing that the goals are simple and not nearly as complicated as you might have thought.

Why and How People Learn

TRADITIONAL LEARNING THEORIES

Just the word "theory" conjures up the image of boredom. So what we are going to do here is paraphrase the traditional learning theories with our apologies to all those educational theorists who have so diligently observed the masses and provided us with their view of why people learn. Each theory presented must be applied to diving or it has little practical value for our purposes. The thing that you should pay attention to is the common thread that weaves its way through each theory.

You will find that there is some truth and application for each theory. You will probably even find yourself reflecting back on teachers who you had at different times in your life and thinking, "so that's what they were doing." Or, you might say, "no wonder I couldn't learn anything from that geek."

The information here was best expressed in the book *Educational Psychology in the Classroom*, by Henry Clay Lindgren, a professor of psychology at San Francisco State College. Professor Lindgren discussed eight "traditional" theories on why people learn. I will relate them as best I can to scuba instruction. See if you can identify the common thread that I spoke of earlier.

■ *REWARD AND PUNISHMENT.* Simply put, this theory holds that people learn that for which they are rewarded, and learn not to do that for which they are punished. There is a lot of truth to this theory, especially with children and small animals. If you reward someone for doing something right, you set up a conditioned response: do it right, get a reward. The same is true for punishment. It too is a conditioned response. If you do something wrong you are punished, so to avoid punishment, don't do anything wrong. Easy, huh? The problem I see here is that after the child grows up, there are lots of potential problems with this simplistic approach. For one thing, one person's reward may be another's punishment, and the other way around.

For example, say you have a student who performs a skill exactly right. So you single that person out for praise and as a reward (in your mind) you ask that person to demonstrate the skill for the class. The problem is that the person is extremely shy and is horror stricken at the prospect of being humiliated in front of the class (his or her view).

What have you accomplished? The exact opposite you were hoping for. It's likely that the student will now withdraw and make sure that they don't do anything special in the future. They would rather risk failure than suffer the pain of being put on exhibition again.

Learning not to put your hand in the fire or step in front of a car are life lessons we learn to avoid trouble. The same is true of many parts of learning to dive. Things like checking to make sure you have plenty of air before diving, not touching certain things, not bumping your head on the boat when you ascend—are all learned in order to avoid some negative consequence. All important and all true. But not the primary reason people learn, and not the best way to teach. People learn because they see a need to know the information. In the cases mentioned, the need is clear and simple: survival. Your job is to make sure the need is always apparent and the message is always simple.

■ **ADDITIVE THEORY** holds that the mind is a sort of storehouse for facts. The more facts you put into it, the more you know and are able to use. Maybe so, maybe not!

In the sense that we are bombarded with information every minute, and that to a certain extent we tend to file that information away somewhere and rely on it to help us make decisions when need be, this theory is reality. But just because we have accumulated lots of information doesn't automatically assure us that we can use it, or even apply it in context when the need arises.

In order for the information to be usable, it has to be applied to something relevant. It must relate to our everyday activity in a way that says "you need to know that so you can be safer and avoid a problem later." If it doesn't, we retain only part, and soon forget that.

In the case of diving, there are areas of information that may not seem important to the student; in fact, they may even be boring. One example may be the Repetitive Dive Tables. But, if you can make them understand the reason they are so important to their safety, they become more than just facts dumped on top of facts, and are now things they need to know.

■ **LEARNING IS PERMANENT** states that if something is properly learned, which implies that it was properly taught, it cannot and will not be forgotten. This theory, on first blush would seem to be utter bunk. However, let's not rush to judgment. There are certainly many lessons in life that we learn and never seem to forget. Like not putting your hand in the fire. But for the most part, unless we can apply those lessons on a daily basis, we tend to lose them. Take the case of a person who speaks a second language fluently, but after years of non-use, simply forgets it. Oh, they may be able to retrieve it with less effort than if they had to learn again from scratch, but it isn't there to use at will.

Much of what we learn in scuba is habit. Nothing more than the repetition of an act until it becomes "learned." If the habit is ingrained deeply enough in our mind, then it does become more or less permanent. Especially if we don't interject options to the habit that may confuse the issue under stress. But for those lessons to become "permanent," we must have a reason to remember them. A clear need to know the information.

■ *BEING TOLD THEORY* means that if you are told something it now is learned. This makes several assumptions, and is part and parcel of both the *additive theory* and the *learning is permanent theory*. Both are based on memorization and assume a permanent accumulation of information that is always available for use.

Just think back on all of your schooling, all of the information you have been exposed to, and see how much of it you recall. Sure there is a lot that remains, but there is also a lot that doesn't.

In scuba training, you can't assume that just because people were exposed to the information ensures that they understood and will be able to apply the information. At one time the universal gas law was taught in scuba courses as a standard subject. It was so abstract and complicated that all but those with a physics background became hopelessly lost. Dedicated individuals might have absorbed enough to get by the exam, but only the rarest of persons retained anything of use past the end of the course. The problem? There was no practical application for the information. It was nothing more than a mathematical explanation of why we absorb gas under pressure and why we release it when pressure is removed (short version). With no clear need to know the universal gas law, it offered no value and was eventually dropped from use by all but the hardest core old-time instructors.

■ *LEARNING AS A STEP-BY-STEP PROCESS* tends to see learning as a predetermined pattern. That is, you start at A and progress through Z and people will learn because of the order of presentation.

There is little question that people learn little things first and that it makes the learning of bigger things much easier. In some cases it is what makes the learning of the bigger thing possible. This is especially true in the teaching of scuba. There are many skills that are learned faster and perfected more quickly if they are preceded by smaller, easier-to-accomplish lessons. An example of this would be mask clearing. When a person has difficulty mastering the technique, it is usually because they are afraid they will run out of air before they get the mask cleared, and believe they will get water up their nose if they attempt to breathe. No amount of reassurance will overcome that fear. However, if they are taught first to breathe through a snorkel without having a mask on, both concerns go away, and they can generally clear a mask the first time.

There are many examples of learning in a step-by-step way throughout diving instruction, not the least of which is the natural progression from shallow confined water to deeper confined water, to shallow open water, to deeper open water where real diving is done. Living is a step-by-step process and learning is just a part of living. Never forget though that how well the lesson is learned is always dependent on how the learner views their personal need to know the information.

■ *AUTOMATIC TRANSFER OF TRAINING THEORY* means just what it says. This theory implies that information and training received in one area automatically transfers to another unrelated area. Well, let's just see about that.

According to the big shoe manufacturers that make cross-training shoes, there must be something to the theory. Certainly if you are physically competent in one sport you are likely to be physically capable in another sport. But, I suggest that probably has more to do with your basic physical ability than automatic transfer of training.

This theory is more relevant to how you think than to what you think. There are many subjects you are exposed to in school, such as geometry or logic, that have almost as much to do with *teaching you how to think* as they do with the subject itself. Learning how to approach a subject in a logical, orderly manner that helps you to see the essence of the topic, may also allow you to learn other subjects faster and more completely. So in the sense that in learning one subject, you have also learned how to approach another unrelated subject, the automatic transfer of training may apply and be correct. Certainly there are many overlapping areas of information, such as physics, that are directly applicable to scuba. Whether the study of English literature has any direct crossover value in the study of scuba diving is another story.

If a student understands how to think, they will begin to understand why the information or skill is important. If they understand how it works, they are much more likely to grasp it quickly and master it for future use. Again, they must have a clear need to know the material.

■ *LEARNING SHOULD BE PAINFUL* doesn't mean that it should physically hurt, it means that it should be difficult and the learner should agonize over the process. The idea being that if it is emotionally painful enough, the learner will be more likely to remember it.

Like all of the above, there is some kernel of truth to the theory. It sure seems to me that the subjects I worked hardest on in school were the most memorable. On the other hand, there were other subjects I enjoyed, worked less hard at, and still retain today to a greater extent than some "harder" courses that I have never really used since.

In the training of scuba divers, I think it's best to remember that the students aren't there because the have to be, they are there because they want to be. And the reason they chose to be there in the first place is because they thought that diving looked like a lot of fun. I ask you, how much fun would it be if the learning process had to be a painful one? Oops, another silly question!

Sometimes, in the pursuit of the mastery of a skill, extra effort is required that at the moment may seem somewhat painful. But the mastery of every skill is important to the safe practice of scuba diving, and the extra effort is not only worthwhile, but is also essential to the future well-being of the individual. The trick for the instructor is to create a balance between the feeling of pain, and the instructor's efforts to make the experience as pleasant as possible. It's all in the attitude. If you make it painful, it will be. If you find a way to make it okay to have some fun and enjoy the process, it will be fun. Sort of like the difference between, "tonight you *have* to get in the pool with a tank and regulator and swim 40 laps under water," and "tonight I'm going to *let* you get into the pool with a tank and regulator, and if you do it right, I'll let you swim up to 40 times around the pool." Like I said, it's all in the attitude. Also, if you added something like "and the ability to make 40 laps around the pool is a great indicator to how safe you will be in the open water," you may also have given them a clear need to know. It could happen!

■ *LEARNING SHOULD BE PLEASANT* is pretty much the opposite of *learning should be painful*. This theory says that every learning experience should be a happy one. A feel good, self-esteem builder.

While I certainly believe that learning should be as pleasant as you can make it, that doesn't mean it sometimes can't be just a little painful. In many cases, learning means change as much as it can mean actually learning something new. Change can mean stress, and stress is an everyday part of living and growing.

Anything in life that is worth having is worth earning. And earning something means that you have to pay your dues. You need to work enough and worry enough so that at the end of the day you can say you really accomplished something. It wasn't given to you, or glossed over to protect your self-esteem. You earned it. The fact that the earning process wasn't all that painful is beside the point. It doesn't take pain, it takes work. Don't ever get the two confused.

Learning is almost always pleasant when it is information we want and need. I believe the human mind craves information. How many people would voluntarily pay money to attend a scuba course unless they were interested and wanted to learn how to dive. By the very act of signing up they told you that much. It is then up to you to provide them with a clear need to know the material you will cover, and to make the journey as pleasant and rewarding for them as possible, while making sure they earn every bit of what they accomplish.

A CLEAR "NEED TO KNOW"

By this time I'm sure you have picked up on the common thread I was weaving through the previous paragraphs. The message should be crystal clear by now. If a person is going to learn to the fullest possible extent, above all else, there must be a clear need for them to know and retain the information.

While I don't think you can overstate the need to know part, it is possible that it may be misinterpreted or overdone if not applied in a thoughtful manner. So let's chew on the real meaning of "need to know" and see if we can give it some balance in the scheme of things.

Virtually everything we learn in life is based on someone's idea of what we need to know. All through school we take subjects that experience has shown to be important to us as adults. Since no one can look into your future and know just what your interests or aptitudes will be, you are presented with a wide spectrum of subjects that have shown themselves to be relevant over a long period of time. These subjects work in concert with life's lessons to create a path down which you will travel depending on your interests and aptitudes. The problem is that you can't always see the value in the subjects they have chosen for you, and even worse, all too often they can't really give you any acceptable reason why.

For whatever reason, certain things are just more interesting to some people than to others. They have some inner need to know about the subject and a strong desire to do so. As a result, they will apply themselves to the pursuit of that information, and typically will learn more and retain it better.

In my teen years I loved cars, and thought I wanted to be an auto mechanic. I couldn't see the need for English classes if I was going to be a mechanic, but I was blessed with a wonderful teacher who made me want to learn. I think the need to know was based on my academic life and death, but in fact, she made it make sense, and showed me that the ability to communicate was critical to my success no matter what I chose to do in the future. I wound up with a degree in Commercial Art, opened a chain of retail stores, have now written several books, and all I do with cars is drive them. Go figure. It really makes me wonder sometimes what direction I would have gone if other teachers had been able to show me a clear need to know the subjects they were teaching. In retrospect, I can now see that everything I was exposed to had value, and each divergent subject might have lead me down a different path.

All any of this really means to you as an instructor of scuba diving, is that each person you deal with is faced with the same kind of questions we all have when we approach a new subject. What do I need to know this for? All I really want to do is get in the water and swim around. I don't want to be a scientist, I just don't want to get into trouble. Show me how to use the gear, and I'm out of here.

While I can't say that things won't change—because you know they will—I can say that in the teaching of scuba, the information has been refined to the point that there is very little if any fluff. Virtually everything presented has a reason to be there. To be a safe diver, the student needs to know it all. So your job is to provide the rationale for every student. You can't just conjure up a single concept or even a series of concepts that will work for every student. Each person has their own reasons, and you must find that reason and provide them with a clear need to know.

DEVELOPING MENTAL AND PHYSICAL SKILLS

Now that we've covered the really exciting theories of how people learn, let's take a look at how people train their bodies to do what they ask of them. Understanding how the students develop their mental and physical skills is an important step in becoming a top-notch instructor, and there is a great deal more to it than meets the eye. Interestingly enough, there has been quite a bit of research done on how the mind trains the muscles to respond. Once you see how this works, you're going to say, "Oh yeah, I've done that." You just didn't know what was happening.

■ *PSYCHO-CYBERNETICS* is a field of study concerning how the mind works in concert with your muscles to develop physical skills. Now that is a gross simplification of a complicated area of study, but descriptively accurate nonetheless. In his book *Psycho-cybernetics*, Maxwell Maltz, M.D., F.I.C.S., details his method for using the mind's ability to create either positive or negative images in your perception of what is happening in your life. It is his technique for creating a positive reinforcement of your experiences and improving your self-image and capacity to learn.

There are two areas of interest to me that this study pointed out. One has to do with the positive reinforcement process, and the second has to do with how the mind is able to train the muscles to respond in order to create a "muscle memory."

Positive reinforcement as applied here is one of the phenomena of human nature that I find fascinating. It is something most of us do without even thinking about it. Unfortunately, there are some people who dwell on the negatives and go through life with a very low sense of self-worth.

A great example of positive reinforcement can be found in your own everyday life. Think about whenever you have tried something new. Something that required physical dexterity. Say a new game of skill. You watched someone else doing the skill, then when you thought you were ready, you decided to try it yourself. Sometimes you were ready and were able to perform the skill the first or second time you tried. But more often than not, you may have failed to do it correctly and needed to step back and watch some more. At that point two things happened if you had a positive attitude. The first was that your mind down-played the negatives of failure and began to focus on the positive things you did. Next, it began to reassess the process and build on the positives until you felt you were ready to try again. Each time you tried you improved until eventually you got it right. Happily, most people approach this kind of situation in the described fashion. The positive person says "I failed to do it this time, I'll try again," kind of like "almost, but not quite." The negative person says "I'm a failure" and gives up.

In scuba instruction we do the same thing, maybe without realizing it. We have students in a class who don't quite catch on to the skill we ask them to perform. You would think that logic alone would tell the instructor that you can't ask a person to go on to a more difficult skill until they have mastered the previous one, but all too often the instructor is in a hurry to get the class completed and misses a critical step in the learning process. The student needs the opportunity to experience the positive reinforcement that time and reflection permit.

When given the chance to step away from a minor set-back, such as not executing a skill the way the instructor wanted, the individual begins to eliminate the negative parts and to reinforce the positives. They then think through how the skill should have been performed and begin to program their muscles to do it correctly.

Dr. Maltz cites the example of three groups of people learning to shoot a basketball. The groups were measured on their first and last days of the experiment. Group one actually shot baskets and improved 24% by the last day. Group two didn't do anything and showed no improvement by the last day (now there's a big surprise). Group three never shot a basket, but was given detailed information about how, and was asked to visualize the actual process. At the end of the test period group three had improved by 23%. Virtually no different than the group that actually shot the baskets.

The student needs the time between classes to step back from the lesson, even if it's only overnight, to suppress the negatives and give the positives a chance to surface. Also, it gives them a chance to think through the skill and let their mind program their muscles to perform it correctly. None of this can be achieved in a so-called short course (a course that is conducted in an intense one- or two-day period). People, even the ones that do everything correctly, just don't have the time for positive reinforcement.

Don't rush the students through, give them a chance to let the natural learning process work. They need the time to give themselves the positive reinforcement, and for their brains to instill the muscle memory needed to be successful. Even the slowest learners will respond if given time. I guess the question for the instructor is, do you want to get the class over with, or do you want to be a successful teacher? I wonder what the answer to that one is?

■ *HABIT BUILDING* is a key part of the process when learning to dive safely. Everybody knows that good habits are better than bad ones, so the idea here is to make safety and good diving procedure a habit.

You don't think about them, or question them; you just do them because that was the way you were taught and because they work.

There are lots of things that people can learn to do and not to do if they are just taught to do the right thing from the start. In scuba diving, this means everything from equipment care to keeping a log book. If you require a certain routine for dressing, preparing your equipment for the dive and so forth, and do it every time, in every class without exception, by the time the course is over it will have become a habit. You will continue to do it the same way for ever more.

It isn't any different than putting on a seat belt in the car. It's real important to your safety, and once you get used to doing it and it becomes habit, you wouldn't even consider driving without one.

For obvious reasons, at least I hope they're obvious, you must be very careful not to let the student practice bad habits. They'll also do them for ever more, and that's not what you want. Since I'm already using driving comparisons, it makes me think of the person who gets in the habit of not quite stopping at the stop sign, it's only a matter of time until they make a mistake and cause some kind of accident.

There are some things in diving that just seem to be natural. That is, a person will tend to do them without being told and they can become a habit. Swimming on the back is one of those things. Not that swimming on your back is inherently wrong, it's just that it won't work for very long under the worst possible conditions. And for any skill to be valid, it has to be able to stand that test. It must work under the worst possible conditions.

People need to be trained to swim on their stomach. It isn't a natural position, and it goes against their instincts to put their face in the water. But it only requires repetition until it becomes natural. Even then, people will roll over and swim on their backs if you don't watch them. "So what?" you might ask. "What's the big deal?" The big deal is that when you are on your back in rough seas, you have a problem with direction control; and even worse, if you use up the leg muscles required to swim on your back, you have also used up the muscles needed to swim on your stomach.

Another example is the simple habit of putting the mask down around your neck, instead of up on your forehead when you are on the surface of the water. A mask on the forehead can be swept away in heavy seas, and the loss of a mask pretty much ends the dive, not to mention the potential for trouble.

So be careful what habits you intentionally or unintentionally establish in your students. The good ones will serve them well, but the bad ones may create problems, even put their lives at risk.

■ *CONDITIONED RESPONSE* is a major key to the proper training of animals, small children, and scuba divers. Some people actually have trouble separating these three groups, but I think the dependability of animals is pretty well documented. As for the human side which has the ability to reason, the very fact that they can reason is why conditioned response is critical to their well-being. In chapter three I'll get into to the actual dynamics of the process, but for now let's just say that trying to reason through an actual emergency can be a disaster. When you must react to a situation and make the right choice or suffer the consequences, you don't want to lock yourself up sorting through options. You need a right thing to do the first time, every time. That kind of response comes only from repetition of the one right choice over and over until it becomes a conditioned response

■ *SUMMARY.* Knowing why people learn is one big step toward becoming a fine teacher. I hope you understand I don't have the room here, nor is it the purpose of this book to attempt to detail every concept about why and how people learn. The fact is, I don't know *all* the ways. But, if you will apply the spirit of what has been presented here, I believe you will understand the basic learning process and be more patient with your students, and hopefully—give them the time they need to become good divers.

Why People Don't Learn

The truth is, if I really knew all the answers to why people don't learn, I could pretty much name my price for the information. There are so many reasons why people don't absorb information that there may be more reasons than people. However, having said that, most of the so-called reasons are nothing more than what has been stated earlier in the chapter. They just don't see the need for it, so they don't care. Or, at least they aren't interested.

The best we can do here is address the problem of why people don't learn in a scuba course, which you wouldn't think would be a problem. After all, they must want to be there because they paid their money. And they must see at least some need for the training or why would they bother to sign up in the first place.

Once a person is in the course, their reasons for not learning tend to be a little easier to figure out than in everyday life. For the instructor, these reasons are what I call *barriers to learning*. The list of barriers is fairly short. There may be others that are yet to be identified, or are unique to some particular students, but the following cover most of the reasons people have problems learning during the course.

■ *APPREHENSION (A.K.A. FEAR)* can be a really big barrier. When someone is afraid, there is very little on their mind but survival. Certainly not whatever lesson you may think is important. The fear is typically from one of two primary causes: either a lack of understanding or a lack of confidence—and sometimes both.

A lack of understanding generally means that the student, like all sensible people, has a healthy fear of what they don't understand. They need to be aware of what is going to happen. Don't ask them to take much on faith. They also need to know how things work. That is, just how a skill is done and what they should expect along the way. They may also have some fear of water they picked up as a kid. Lots of people carry that one around. Happily, if you can help them relax in the water to start with, once they start swimming around with scuba gear, they realize that their fears were groundless (no pun intended).

There are many reasons why people lack confidence. They may be unsure of themselves. A surprisingly large number of the people who sign up for lessons didn't think through just what was involved. Once the class begins they may question their own abilities, if for no other reason than that they haven't been in the water for awhile.

It isn't at all unusual for someone who doesn't know how to swim to sign up for lessons. That can be a pretty big barrier! The good news is that a common reason people can't swim is because they are afraid of what's *in* the water. Just like the person who knows how to swim but was afraid of the water itself. Once they start swimming with equipment on and can actually see under water, they lose their fear and are eager, or at least willing, to learn how to swim without the equipment.

■ *COLD* is a major killer of the mind. Not on a conscious level, it is much more subtle than that. Mentally, cold creeps into your subconscious and actually slows down your ability to think. You start to shiver with the onset of hypothermia, and before you know it you are so involved in freezing that any hope of learning something is gone.

Physically, cold slows your reactions and makes it difficult, if not impossible, to perform the skills properly. The instructor needs to guard against letting the students get chilled. Don't put them in the water until you need to, and don't let them stand around too much. Keep them moving, and if possible, put them in some kind of protective suit. If they're warm they will learn faster and have a lot more fun.

■ *INADEQUATE EQUIPMENT* has a major effect on learning because it creates a distraction, raises the student's stress level, and inhibits their ability to deal with mechanical skills as well.

If the equipment isn't up to the job, the student begins to focus on the problem rather than the lesson. A regulator that leaks or doesn't breathe right is a major distraction. Soon the stress level starts up and not only keeps the student from learning, but creates a potential safety problem as well. If the student is preoccupied with some equipment problem, they may not see another problem developing. They lack the experience to deal with surprises and are always on the edge of a potential problem. Make sure that they always have enough of the right equipment and that it is in good working order. This will remove another barrier to learning.

■ *POOR ADJUSTMENT OF EQUIPMENT* has many of the same problems associated with it that inadequate equipment does. The problem though is not so obvious as a leaky regulator.

When a student is constantly fussing with their equipment because it is poorly adjusted, they aren't paying attention to you. But even worse, they may be heading for trouble, both in the short term and when they start to dive on their own. In the short term, poorly adjusted equipment can be a catalyst for the psycho-respiratory cycle. This is covered in some detail later, but what it means is that problems can initiate stress which can lead to hyperventilation. If not stopped, panic can be close behind. Even if none of this happens, it is always a barrier to the learning process. Of real concern is that in the long run, if people don't develop the habit of proper adjustment, they run the risk of safety problems every time they dive.

■ *STRESS*, like cold, can completely stop the learning process. When a person is under stress from some outside source, it can become the most important thing in their life. It will dominate their every thought. Now you can't always do much about some degree of outside stressor, but you can control how much stress is created within the course of scuba instruction.

When a student is stressed because of the skills they are asked to perform, they spend more time worrying about whether they can do the skill than how it is done. You must remove that concern and put them at ease. If stress is allowed to continue, the person will become anxious. The anxiety will begin to increase the respiratory level, and the person will be headed for trouble. As mentioned, this cycle will be detailed later in the book, but it should be obvious that you don't want that process to get started. It can be controlled by simply being aware of the person's reactions, and stopping them if you notice the onset of anxiety. Let them relax and help them understand that learning is not a test, but a chance to develop new skills. Sometimes it takes a little while to perfect the skills and they should just calm down and enjoy the process.

■ **PHYSICAL CONDITIONING** isn't usually a problem until it becomes one. How's that for a profound statement? What I mean is, if you are out of shape you can still perform most of what is required to learn how to dive. After all, diving really isn't that physically difficult, and if you relax and enjoy the process, it puts very little strain on you.

There are, however, two problems to consider. The first has to do with learning. If the physical effort becomes troublesome for the student, they will become more concerned about their well-being than the lesson. So being physically prepared for the course is a major aid to the learning process and eliminates another barrier.

The second problem has to do with what happens if the person exceeds their physical ability and puts themself in a life-threatening situation. The first problem is merely a barrier to learning, the second is a matter of life and death. You must impress on your students that diving is sometimes a rigorous activity, and they need to maintain a level of physical ability that permits them to deal with a problem should it arise.

■ **THE INSTRUCTOR** should be part of the solution, not part of the problem. You can do this by setting good behavioral objectives. Help the student form good habits and a clear knowledge about themself.

Remove as many barriers as you possibly can. Don't worry too much about the outside influences unless they are something you can fix. Concentrate on not creating any of the common barriers we have talked about.

Handle all the tough problems yourself. Don't make the common mistake of passing off problem students to an assistant. The person with the problem is the one who needs your expertise. The assistant can handle all the people who can do everything the first time. Don't forget, the challenge and the joy of teaching lies with helping the ones who don't get it. Anyone can tell a gifted person what to do and watch them do it. It requires real skill on the part of the instructor to train the apparently untrainable.

■ *ATTITUDE* is one of the major barriers. Naturally I'm referring to a *bad* attitude. A bad attitude can develop for any number of reasons— a spouse that doesn't want to be there, a dominating boyfriend, a parent or friend, or a million other things. Maybe worse is the person who comes to the class with some diving background and thinks he or she is King Neptune. It can be especially bad if they turn out to be no-talent jerks. There can be an endless list of reasons why people have an attitude. It is your job to discover the source and overcome it.

The reality is that attitude is usually a cover-up for insecurity. So, if the people don't feel threatened by you and come to understand that you are their friend and really want to see them succeed, they will generally respond in kind. Show them that you really like them. One thing is for sure, it is nearly impossible to dislike someone who openly likes you.

■ *SUMMARY.* Tear down the barriers when you find them, and try never to be the cause of any. Most of the problems the people bring with them can be overcome with understanding and patience. Time and a caring attitude from you will almost always result in removing that barrier.

It is entirely up to you to make sure that you don't unintentionally create barriers such as letting them get too cold, or not providing enough of the right equipment, or failing to make sure their equipment is properly adjusted. Start things off right and help them build good habits by doing the right thing, and by eliminating any and all barriers to learning.

USING MULTI-MEDIA

When you cut through all of the theories and scientific mumbo-jumbo about the learning process, it seems to boil down to the fact that people learn easier when they have a reason to learn, and they don't learn as well when they don't have a reason, or if you allow too many barriers to develop in the process. However, even when the conditions are perfect and they want to learn, and they understand the need, and all the barriers are gone, there is still the fact that people tend to process information in their own way.

Some learn better when they hear or see, some when they do or say, and others by a combination of these. In fact, such things have been measured, and according to research done at the University of Texas, people tend to retain information based on the following:

- 10% OF WHAT THEY *READ*
- 20% OF WHAT THEY *HEAR*
- 30% OF WHAT THEY *SEE*
- 50% OF WHAT THEY *HEAR* AND *SEE*
- 70% OF WHAT THEY *SAY*
- 90% OF WHAT THEY *SAY* AS THEY *DO* A THING

Now, before we all get too excited about these numbers, understand that these are possibles, not for-sures. That is to say, if everything went perfectly, and the person was in all ways capable, they could learn up to the percentages indicated. However, in a scuba course the conditions will rarely if ever be optimal.

As I mentioned earlier, you are faced with all ages, intellectual abilities, and interest levels. For this reason, you must make your best effort to cover all the bases, and to do it several times. That means that in addition to multi-media, you must also include other meaningful repetition of the material (the key word here is meaningful).

Multi-media can mean different things to different people. What I mean is information from a variety of sources such as text books, workbooks, video, lecture, practical application, and a testing procedure to ensure that the student "got it."

To maximize the effectiveness of the various methods of presentation, it is generally most effective if you can alternate the passive and active sources.

Some kinds of information come from a passive source, as when you are *told* something. Others are active, as when we actually *do* something. By alternating between the two, the student has the chance to hear how it is done, and then try it. As they return to the passive mode, they have a chance to step away from the active and let their minds perform some positive reinforcement—remember the psycho-cybernetics?

By utilizing different media, the student is given the opportunity to read, see, hear, and then do, so they are exposing all of their senses. And, if each of the media forms repeats the vital information, and then the instructor combines that with further repetition in the practical part of the course, you have bombarded the student from every conceivable direction. Further, assuming that the information was understandable in the first place, they should have had ample opportunity to learn what they needed to know.

■ *SUMMARY.* Let's review what we've covered so far. If you expect to teach in an effective way, you need to understand *why* people learn. Hopefully you now know that if they are going to retain the information, they must have a clear need to know why the information is important to their well-being.

You must also understand why people *don't* learn. There are a great many barriers to the learning process, and your job is to discover what *their* barriers are, help them past those barriers, and be sure not to put up any barriers of your own.

Finally, you must understand that people learn from many sources. Each person has the ability to absorb information from one source better than from another. Your job is to cover the bases. Present the information from every conceivable direction, repeat the meaningful information during the practical part of the training, and then give them ample time to practice until the skill becomes a conditioned automatic response.

It isn't my intent to bog you down with detailed explanations about the various scientific theories. There are many sources for long and often tedious explanations of how the researchers arrived at their conclusions, and the resulting case histories. My intent has been to apply that information, in a practical way, to the challenge of teaching scuba diving. The specifics of teaching the courses are being left up to the training agencies that design them.

CHAPTER 2

Preventative Training

Preventative training is how you teach the new diver to dive defensively, and defensive diving is the single most important concept for keeping the diver safe in the long term.

In order to teach preventative diving, you as the instructor must first understand how and why accidents happen. Only then can you properly explain and justify the habit-building process the student must go through in order to be prepared to dive defensively.

The ability to truly dive defensively can be likened to becoming a good driver in a car. First you learn how to actually operate the automobile, then you learn the rules of the road and you think you are ready to hit the streets. In reality, there is a big difference between knowing how to steer and brake, and actually being prepared for the weirdness of all the other drivers on the road. To be a safe driver you have to learn to anticipate all the stupid things that other drivers do from time to time. That process is called *defensive driving*.

It is much the same in diving. You learn how to use the equipment, then apply that knowledge to open water. That's like learning to steer and brake. Next you must learn how not to get into trouble, just like learning about the weird drivers. That's what preventative training is all about—learning why and how accidents happen so you know what to avoid. Finally, defensive diving is putting together all that knowledge and using it to recognize when a problem is developing, or when a situation has danger written all over it.

If you can teach people never to get into trouble in the first place, the probability of an accident is much, much less. Sure, there are still things that can happen that are out of the diver's control. One example would be something that someone else does to you, like pulling you under water before you're ready.

In the ocean there are times when conditions change from what they were when the dive started and when you first made your dive plan. Tides shift, winds come up, boats break down, currents carry you too far, and other things happen that can change the nature of the dive and require alteration of the plan. When something changes, or you get a nasty surprise like equipment failure—which thankfully doesn't happen too often—you have to be prepared to change the plan and deal with the surprise.

There really aren't that many different causes of diving accidents, at least not of the type we can prevent. They usually stem from poor preparation, equipment problems (not failure), a lack of preventative skills, an unforeseen emotional development, misuse of drugs, or sickness.

To be sure, there are things that can happen that aren't listed, but the vast majority seem to fall under one of these categories. So we're going to examine each one and see why accidents happen and learn how to prevent them by diving defensively.

Causes of Diving Accidents

POOR PREPARATION

As with everything in life, preparation is the key to success. Without it you're just flipping a coin about the outcome, and—more often than not—the outcome would have been pretty obvious if you had just thought about it. Poor preparation is kind of like the guy who takes a knife to a gun fight: his hopes for success just aren't that great.

■ *CONDITIONING*, or more correctly a lack thereof, is a big contributor to diving accidents. I mentioned earlier that diving is a sport that can be done by someone who's not in very good physical condition. If everything goes perfectly, with no surprises, the equipment available today will permit such a person to dive. The problem is that if *anything* goes wrong, they may be in deep trouble.

To be physically prepared to dive, you've got to maintain a level of fitness that allows you to deal with problems as they arise. Notice I said *as* they arise—not *if*. There are too many unforeseen potential problems awaiting the unprepared diver for them to really believe they will never hit a snag.

There are three main conditioning problems that appear to be the areas of greatest concern: being out of shape, being overweight, and smoking.

- Being out of shape is what we have just been discussing. It is vital that your students are physically prepared for the open water. They may not be in great shape when they start a class, but they should be in adequate shape by the time they are ready for their open water classes or, at the very latest, by the time they get certified. You may not be able to control what happens once they are out on their own, but you can ensure they don't have problems on your watch.

  Don't be surprised if people show up for their first class in poor shape. They don't always realize how important it is. Just for clarification here, when I talk about being in shape I don't mean you have to be a body builder or an olympic athlete. I'm simply referring to the ability to survive: being able to swim a few laps of the pool, being able to tread water—things like that. And, they should be able to do them without having a coronary. Anyway, the point is they may show up in poor condition, but you have ample time to get them into better shape. Have them swim some easy laps with their fins and mask on during each pool session. It's no big deal, but you'll be surprised how quickly they shape up.

- Weight problems are kind of touchy. People who are heavy know they are and don't really need you to remind them. Also, since the water tends to buoy them up, sometimes they're more comfortable in the water than out. I've personally known several great divers over the years that were quite a bit overweight.

Unfortunately, there are problems that seem to occur more often in overweight people than in those who aren't. Heart attacks leap to mind, but there are others as well. Overweight people should be aware of the potential for problems so they can make an informed decision about how they want to dive. Your job is to be helpful and informative, not to judge whether someone is too heavy by your standards.

- Smokers are in a class by themselves. I don't mean to sound preachy or judgmental, but it seems to me that there is plenty of evidence that smoking is bad for your health, and that people wouldn't consciously choose to put their bodies through that kind of torture.

When it comes to diving, there is also the problem of water pressure and lung expansion to consider. Smokers' lungs just aren't very healthy. They lack the elasticity of the non-smoker's lungs, and there are enough opportunities for over-expansion to occur that smoking is a very real threat to these people.

It isn't likely that anything you say or do will make a smoker quit, and you'll only create problems by nagging. So I suggest that you simply inform the person of the potential problems and let them decide. It's their life and how they live it is up to them. Your job is to make sure they understand the potential ramifications.

■ *LACK OF PROPER TRAINING* is a huge contributor to diving accidents. There are way too many people that were given their certification based on the fact that they "got through" the course. They performed every skill the instructor asked them to, but maybe just barely. They weren't comfortable or confident, but they did it.

People who don't feel good about their skills generally just quit the sport after certification. That's good news for their future safety, but bad news for the sport and a real poor commentary about someone's teaching ability. Once in a while these unprepared people actually try to go diving, and they are an accident waiting to happen.

They have poor reactions to unexpected problems, and they're too busy fussing with things to anticipate problems before they arise.

You don't do the student or yourself a favor by sending them out unprepared. Your best advertising is a happy customer, and your worst is an unhappy one, not to mention that certifying a person who isn't truly ready is an unprofessional thing to do.

■ *LACK OF REQUIRED KNOWLEDGE* has the same problems and results that a lack of training does. I was referring to a lack of physical skill in the previous paragraphs, but lack of knowledge about how you are affected physically by increasing water pressure, as well as the mechanics of the ocean and the creatures that live there, can put the diver at risk.

The diver must know how to function intellectually in the underwater environment or they stand to be its victim. There are just too many incidents that take place because the diver "just didn't know any better."

Give the people the knowledge they need and teach them to use the tools available. Make sure they have everything they need to be successful.

EQUIPMENT PROBLEMS

It is rare for a piece of diving equipment to fail as a result of a design flaw or a breakdown of a critical part. But it isn't at all uncommon for equipment to malfunction because of improper care or user abuse; nor is it unusual for accidents to happen as a result of misuse or improper adjustment of the equipment.

■ *INADEQUATE EQUIPMENT* can mean that either it wasn't up to the job or there wasn't enough of it. Since there is little if any life-support equipment sold today that is unsafe, inadequate comes to mean that there wasn't enough equipment to ensure safety.

Anytime you enter the water, the increase in water pressure causes changes to your body. Safety demands that you keep track of the changes. If you don't you risk any number of problems, all of which can be dangerous and some of which are potentially life threatening.

There are all kinds of equipment available designed to keep track of everything you need to know to keep yourself safe. If you don't use it you're just rolling the dice, and the dice are loaded.

■ *MISUSE OF EQUIPMENT*, as in not taking care of it, isn't very smart. When your life depends on the unobstructed delivery of air under water, why wouldn't you want to take special care of that device? As I said earlier, almost all the accidents that are equipment related seem to result from misuse or abuse of the equipment.

■ *MALFUNCTION OF EQUIPMENT* is rare and has been pretty well covered by now. It can and has happened, but it's not something to lose sleep over. Just make sure that your equipment and all equipment used by your students is well maintained, and you have little to worry about.

■ *POORLY ADJUSTED OR MISFITTED EQUIPMENT* is another big contributor to diving accidents. It may not be the direct cause, but when the equipment doesn't feel right and the problem isn't taken care of, it causes distractions for the wearer that may result in an accident.

There are lots of adjustments you should pay attention to, like a weight belt that shifts or is too heavy, a wet suit that is too tight, a buoyancy compensator that's too big or too small, loose fins, a mask that leaks...the list can go on and on. They all represent minor irritations that can lead to big problems.

The minor irritations create a distraction to the job at hand. When a diver is constantly fighting the equipment they start to breathe a little harder. That causes their anxiety level to rise, which makes them breathe harder still, which in turn shoots up the anxiety level even further. This is called the *psycho-respiratory cycle*. Any sudden, outside intrusion can trigger a panic attack. It just depends on the person and how they deal with such things. The interesting part is that all they have to do is make sure their equipment fits and is properly adjusted, and the probability of a problem goes away.

FAILURE TO DEVELOP PREVENTATIVE SKILLS

Not teaching a diver how to dive defensively by developing preventative skills would be like teaching someone to drive in an empty field and then sending them out in rush hour traffic. Both the diver and the driver need to be aware of what they are likely to encounter so they can avoid putting themselves in harm's way.

There are several fundamental reasons why people get into trouble if they aren't prepared:

- LACK OF AWARENESS
- LACK OF PREPARATION
- UNFORESEEN DEVELOPMENTS
- DRUG USE

Like everything in life, if you understand what the potential problems are and know how to avoid them, you stand a better chance of not getting into trouble.

■ *LACK OF AWARENESS* about how accidents happen can let you swim right into one. I want to make sure you understand why they happen so you can help your students understand too.

Let's face it, if you don't know something can be a problem, it's pretty hard to avoid it. On the other hand, once you know that something has the potential for trouble and dive defensively, you rarely put yourself in harm's way. An example would be if you were diving along a reef and saw a hole that could easily be home for a moray eel, you (hopefully) wouldn't stick your hand in to see if one was in there. Common sense would dictate that there might be, and it would guide you to proceed with due caution. (It's a real bad idea to stick your hand uninvited into a moray's home. They don't like that any more than you would—and they tend to bite back!)

■ *LACK OF PREPARATION* is another contributor to diving accidents. Far too many people have had an accident because they weren't prepared for the conditions, or were unable to react in the right way when something went wrong.

If a diver doesn't make a dive plan that accounts for things like tidal change, they really increase the chance of trouble. It's quite common for people to do things like start their dive close to the water's edge, not realizing that it was low tide, and leave everything on the beach to go diving. In the meantime, the tide comes in, washes away all their stuff, and they surface to find they are now a long, long way from shore.

I witnessed a situation where divers entered the water in an inlet to a bay at slack tide. Before they had even reached their diving spot the tide started in. They were swept away before they could start back. They were experienced divers and no one was hurt, but they wound up over a mile away before they could exit the water. They were very lucky. These examples represent the type of things that can happen unless the diver is aware that they can and is prepared to avoid them.

■ *UNFORESEEN DEVELOPMENTS* can mean almost anything. To me it means surprise occurrences, like the sudden appearance of a shark that maybe scares the heck out of you, losing your air supply unexpectedly, or without warning you suddenly feel sick.

While a diver can't really ever be ready for something like a big shark watching them with what they imagine is a yummy look in its eye, they can assume that every now and then a surprise of some kind is bound to happen. The key to handling those types of situations lies in remaining calm and not overreacting. If the diver panics just because of a little surprise, they are almost certain to make the wrong choice about what to do. Especially when doing nothing is the right choice.

• Happenings like the sudden loss of your air supply are why you practice to develop automatic conditioned responses. You've got to have something to breathe, and if you can't get it through your regulator, the only other place air is available is on the surface. If you aren't prepared for the possibility of this happening, and don't have the proper response etched in your brain, you may very well be like one of those before you who has suffered the consequences of not paying attention in class.

• Getting sick while diving is something that usually results from some kind of excess prior to the dive. A typical scenario would be the person who goes on vacation, stays up late and partys, drinks too much, eats too much, and then goes diving the next day. They don't feel all that good when they get on the boat, and they feel really bad by the time they get to the dive site. But, they've already paid their money and they're going to go diving. Sometimes getting off the boat and into the water helps settle them down, but too often they continue to feel worse and actually get ill under water. If they had just said "I don't feel good and I'm not going to risk getting sick under water," everything would have been fine. Sure, they missed a dive, but they'll get another chance. But once they get sick under water, there are no good things that happen except surviving. Everything else is bad. Dive defensively by assuming that it won't get better, but will probably get worse.

■ **DRUG USE** is one of the most dangerous and insidious causes of diving accidents. I'm not referring just to the use of illegal drugs. There are lots of over-the-counter drugs, as well as alcohol, that can have a profound effect on your well-being.

Any illegal drug should be avoided, for what I hope are obvious reasons, but any drug can become a problem when you go under water. With the increase in pressure, whatever effect the drug produced on the surface is greatly intensified under water, plus it can be far different than you would anticipate on the surface.

Under pressure, some over-the-counter drugs, such as certain decongestants, can produce extreme anxiety in the user. Others, such as some nasal sprays, produce what is called *rebound*. That means that when the drug wears off, the original problem rebounds and is greater than before you used it. If that happens under water and traps compressed air in the diver's ear canals, over-expansion and rupture of the ear drums is a real possibility.

The bottom line is that drugs impair your ability to reason and may have serious side effects under water. They may be the cause of many of the accidents that are initially believed to have happened for some other seemingly more obvious reason. They should be avoided unless you know for sure what the effects will be under pressure.

■ *SUMMARY.* When you consider the ways that a lack of awareness and preparation can affect a diver, or how unforeseen developments such as surprises, getting sick, or drug abuse—even of legal drugs—can impact their safety, your mind is opened to thinking seriously about the absolute need for preventative training.

You also come to realize that it would be nearly impossible to cover every kind of diving accident. In fact, every time the diving community thinks they might be getting a handle on the various causes of accidents, someone goes and finds a new way to mess up. The real point is that the best way to avoid accidents is to dive in a way that prevents them. Learn to dive defensively. Assume that what *can* go wrong, *will* go wrong. That doesn't mean being negative all the time, it simply means being careful and avoiding potential pitfalls by knowing what the pitfalls are.

Building Good Habits

We have been talking about avoiding problems and building good habits, but up to now I haven't been very specific about either how to build good habits or even what habits need to be built.

There are all kinds of habits. If not shown the right ones, students will develop their own, but they may be bad ones. Experience has shown that new divers are a clean slate. They don't really know anything about what to do until you tell them. Start them out the right way and require that they do what you ask over and over, in every class. By the time they are certified, they will have developed the right habits, and they won't question the procedure; they'll do it because they were taught to and they practiced it enough that they won't forget.

There are two basic areas that are involved in establishing good scuba diving habits. They are:

- LEARNING THE RIGHT WAY TO HANDLE EQUIPMENT
- ACQUIRING ENOUGH KNOWLEDGE TO BUILD GOOD DIVING HABITS

These are the preventative skills that can ensure the student will always dive defensively.

GOOD EQUIPMENT HABITS

■ *PROPER EQUIPMENT HANDLING* begins with a clear understanding of what it is you are really trying to accomplish and why. Earlier I alluded to some of the effects of poor equipment skills and how that could contribute to problems. All true, but let me put it into a clear, simple perspective.

Scuba is a fascinating sport, and when you are involved in the activity you rarely think about your equipment. You expect it to function properly, and you take it for granted. During the dive you are so preoccupied with your surroundings that nothing else matters.

It should stand to reason that anything that is out of place in any way becomes a nagging irritation to your subconscious mind while you are so preoccupied. The goal then is to remove any potential distraction that can interrupt the dive or has the potential to become a contributor to a problem. To do that, the diver must make a habit of pre-dive preparation and make sure that every piece of equipment functions, fits correctly, and is properly adjusted.

The pre-dive check is very much like the pre-flight check for a pilot. You are confirming that everything is in its place and works like it should. You begin by making sure you have all of the equipment needed for the dive. Then you assemble it and check to make sure it works.

Next, make any adjustments that may be needed. This includes checking to confirm the correct amount of weight, the placement of the weights on the belt, and that the belt is the right size over the wet suit. Once all the necessary adjustments have been made and everything fits, place the equipment in the order in which it is going to be put on.

There are lots of reasons for all this besides what happens in the water. If the weather is hot or the water is rough, the diver wants to get off the boat as soon as possible. They don't want to be standing around in hot, heavy, equipment waiting for a rocking boat to anchor. If the equipment is laid out in the dressing order, they can dress quite fast and be in the water with a minimum of discomfort, reducing the risk of getting overheated and maybe sick.

The whole idea is to teach your students to develop the habit of getting ready and into the water with as little effort as possible, and with properly adjusted equipment that fits and works as it should. If you do this, one area of potential trouble has been all but eliminated.

HAVING ENOUGH KNOWLEDGE

Diving safely is dependent on being able to put to use all of the different things the student learns during the course of training. In addition to the mechanical skills such as mask clearing, the student must know how to use the equipment to their advantage, know how it works, and equally important, they need to learn about the environment they are preparing to enter. These are the areas of information that will determine whether they have simply learned how to use the equipment or they are really going to be divers.

■ *KNOWING WHAT TO EXPECT* helps the diver to understand why the habits are so important, as well as how they work to prevent accidents.

When you enter the water, the pressure begins to affect your mind and your body. As mentioned earlier, keeping track of the changes is essential to safe diving. But *having* the equipment you need to keep track, and actually *using* it, aren't the same thing. In fact, if you study accident reports, it's alarming to note how many people get into trouble, even when they had the necessary equipment to avoid it. Either they just didn't use it, or didn't trust it, or they abused the information it gave them. Or maybe they just had it and never knew how to use it in the first place. Whatever the reason, if they had developed the habit of good diving procedures, they probably would have avoided trouble.

■ *KNOWING HOW THE EQUIPMENT WORKS* can help the diver recognize when it isn't working right. Sometimes everything seems fine on the surface, but once they get under water they may detect a problem that wouldn't show up on the surface. Problems like a hole in the diaphragm of the second-stage on the regulator, or a leak in a hose or connection, that kind of thing. If the diver knows how the equipment is supposed to work then they are more likely to realize quickly when it doesn't. When they understand more about the equipment, they simply develop the habit of confirming that it functions properly every time they prepare to go diving.

■ *LEARNING ABOUT THE ENVIRONMENT*, because not only can the physical properties of the ocean have a profound effect on the diver, but the diver can have an equally big effect on the ocean.

You wouldn't walk into a fenced yard that had a big and mean looking dog in it. At least not until you knew it was safe. The same is true under water. You are in the yard of every creature in the ocean, and you should respect their home.

Neither would you try to swim *up* a river. So knowing how the ocean works is pretty darned important if you want to make the dive easy and, more importantly, safe.

If you teach your students to make a policy of practicing good habits while they dive—keeping their buoyancy adjusted so they stay off the bottom and being very careful of what they touch—they not only avoid problems for themselves, but they are also protecting a very fragile ecosystem.

■ *PEOPLE AREN'T BULLET-PROOF.* Everyone must know their limitations and make a habit of staying within those limitations. Whether physical or mental, the diver should be very careful about exceeding their comfort level.

Teach divers to make their own decisions about how they like to dive and what kind of conditions they are comfortable with, and *never* let anyone pressure them into doing more than they feel good about. There are always going to be those who live on the edge and take chances as a way of life. Teach them not to do something just because someone else does. They should develop the habit of taking only little steps into the unknown, not big leaps. The surest path to an accident is when you act like nothing can ever happen to you.

■ *SUMMARY.* Teach your students more than just how to handle equipment. Teach them to learn about how things work, and why. Show them what the underwater world is about and help them understand that safe diving is the application of all the knowledge they have gained, and even more, it is the prudent application of that knowledge. *Make safe diving a habit!*

Defensive Diving

Defensive diving is nothing more than the practical application of preventative skills and good diving habits. It is the policy of assuming that if something can go wrong, it probably will, and then applying the skills, habits and common sense to the situation at hand to prevent anything from happening.

There's little question that there are going to be times when the diver will avoid doing something because of its potential for trouble, when in all likelihood, nothing would have happened if they had gone ahead and done it. *But, they couldn't be sure of that!* If they knew absolutely there would be no problem, then there wouldn't be any reason not to go ahead, *but they don't know!*

I'm not suggesting that you train students to be wimps, I'm saying that there is a balance between being reckless and being overly cautious, and if you are going to make the wrong decision, make it on the side of caution. All the training and preparation will make diving a safe, enjoyable sport, but bad judgment can override all of that in the blink of an eye.

There are going to be many situations over a diving career that hold the potential for harm. Some divers will look at the situation and say "no thanks." Others will think it could be a problem, but feel they can handle it and go ahead. However, this will often lead to bad results. Still others won't even hesitate—they will just go blindly ahead, assuming that they can handle anything or that there really isn't any problem. The saddest situations involve the unfortunate ones that are talked into doing something they know they shouldn't.

■ *SUMMARY.* So then, let's recap and identify the common thread in this chapter. If you are going to teach people to dive defensively, *you* must learn about how divers get themselves into trouble and what causes the very few accidents that actually happen. Then teach your students to dive defensively by using their preventative training to keep themselves constantly aware of how *not* to get hurt. Help them build good diving habits that create a defensive mind-set, and make sure they understand how to recognize potential problems before they happen. In short, teach them not to get into trouble in the first place.

CHAPTER 3

Contingency Training

Webster defines contingency as *a possible event*. So, it would logically follow (at least in my mind) that contingency training means preparing for a possible event. In the case of diving, it means being prepared if, despite your best efforts to dive defensively, something still goes wrong. Because if there is one thing we can count on absolutely, it is that you should never say never.

An unfortunate fact of life is that accidents happen. There seem to be forces beyond our control that periodically take over intrude on what we are doing and cause us some kind of problem, regardless of how well we planned and prepared.

When such an event occurs, the best we can hope for is that we are somehow able to react in a manner that successfully overcomes the problem and leaves us safe to reflect on and learn from the experience.

To prepare students to deal with contingencies they first must know that there are two basic kinds of problems: *solvable* ones that allow plenty of time for considering how best to handle them, and *unsolvable* ones that allow no time at all but require an automatic conditioned response.

They must also know that for every problem there are what I call *viable* and *non-viable* options, which to me means that some actions will work to solve the problem, and some won't. The trick is to identify the ones that work and prepare your students to respond to the unsolvable problems with an automatic, conditioned, viable option. Remember, it's not enough just knowing how to respond to an emergency—it is just as important to be able to *recognize* when an emergency exists.

Let's charge ahead and see if we can make some sense of all this.

Identifying Problems

While there are many ways problems can manifest themselves, they all boil down to one of two things. Either you have time to think through the problem and reason out an answer, or events proceed so quickly that there simply isn't time to do anything but react.

The late Dr. Arthur B. Hardy, a noted psychiatrist who researched and developed the initial findings on the treatment of agoraphobia—which is defined as a fear of open spaces but is basically a fear of everything—put the decision-making process and its likely results into clear, concise words. (I know Dr. Hardy will forgive my paraphrasing his research, since in addition to being a brilliant man, he was also my uncle—you know how uncles are with nephews.)

Imagine that you are driving down the road at 75 miles per hour. As you drive along you see a sign that tells you Exit 52, which is your turn, is coming up in 5 miles. There are subsequent signs every mile, until you reach the last sign which reads "Exit 52 next right." You make your turn, no problem. You had plenty of time to get ready and think through what you wanted to do.

Now let's imagine you are driving down that same road at 75 miles per hour, and you round a sharp curve and immediately in front of you are three signs across the road. One of the signs reads "I-80 this lane," a second indicates the next town is the second right, and according to the third sign, Exit 52 is the next right. You have about 4 nanoseconds to read the signs, process the information, and make a decision.

Since there wasn't enough time to make a decision based on reason and logic, you make the first one that time permits you to make. It will probably be the first one that makes an impression on your mind. There is a one-in-three chance that it will be the right one, but it is twice as likely that you will make the wrong one.

Dr. Hardy also noted that there are only two kinds of people. There are those who when faced with a problem will stand and fight, and there are the rest who will turn and run. It's called the *survival instinct*, and it is much stronger in some than in others. This instinct has nothing to do with bravery or cowardice; flight or fight is based strictly on a will to survive.

When you understand how people make decisions under stress, and that time may not permit reason, you have the basis for dealing with a potential problem. When you also know that people will react one of two ways when they believe they are in danger, you now have the foundation needed to create a contingency skill for what could possibly become a problem.

SOLVABLE PROBLEMS

Solvable problems are those that allow time for consideration and a follow-up reaction. Most of life's problems fall under this category (thank goodness), and we normally deal with them so casually that in many instances we may not even realize there was a problem.

In diving, there are two types of solvable problems: the ones you take care of by yourself (independent responses), and the ones that require help from a buddy (dependent responses). Knowing this, you can further develop the diver's thought process so they spend as little time as possible deciding what to do when an emergency arises.

■ *INDEPENDENT RESPONSES* are those that permit the diver to deal with a problem themselves. These would include simple problems like clearing the mask or regulator and making simple adjustments to equipment. It can also include real emergency problems like loss of the air supply.

The loss of the air supply is usually nothing more than an inconvenience, but it has the potential for being the very worst thing that can happen to a diver. I say that because the continued lack of something to breathe under water has only one ending. The answer of course is to get something to breathe as soon as possible. Since we are talking about independent action, the correct response is for the diver to ascend to the surface and breathe natural air. This may seem painfully obvious, but the key to a safe procedure lies with having only one thing to do, one decision to make, and a conditioned response to the problem.

When the diver has plenty of time to think through what their action will be, they can simply make a controlled ascent. As they rise their BC will begin to inflate, so controlling their buoyancy and rate of ascent is very important. Also, the probability is that even though they couldn't get air while on the bottom, they may very well be able to get another breath as they ascend and their air supply expands. Either way, trying to breathe from the regulator on ascent won't create any problem in terms of over-expansion. If the throat is open to allow air in, it is also open to allow air out if the lungs become too full.

The point is that there really isn't that much concern, as long as the diver has time to consider their course of action, and follow that course in a controlled manner. As you will see later, the problem comes when there is no time.

■ *DEPENDENT RESPONSES* are those that require the help of a buddy. Many situations that happen under water would typically be classified as the dependent type even if they could be accomplished independently. That's because it is so much easier to have help than to do something by yourself.

A buddy can make adjustments easier, help you out if you're tired, etc. They're also a great comfort if your air runs low. It's nice to know that another air source is close at hand. They are especially helpful if you should somehow become entangled in a way that makes it difficult—or for some really foolish reason you should be unable—to help yourself.

There are contingency skills which are taught by every agency that are designed to deal with such problems, and you must make sure your students are well prepared to react should the need arise. But once again, dependent responses only work reliably when there is time to stop and consider the course of action. Both the diver and their buddy must be in complete control to perform the procedure required for a safe return to the surface.

UNSOLVABLE PROBLEMS

These are problems that arise from situations that require an automatic, conditioned response due to the immediate onset of a problem. There is no time to waste, because if something isn't done *right now*, the alternative is drowning, which is *not* an alternative. Having said that, it must also be noted that this does not mean thoughtless response. On the contrary, the diver should at all times remain calm and carefully consider what the problem is. However, once they determine that a life-threatening situation exists, they must be able to react without confusion or hesitation.

Emergencies usually develop as the result of either a physical problem such as exhaustion, a mechanical problem such as a loss of their air supply, or an emotional problem brought on by stress from any number of things.

Regardless of the cause, the response must be the same. There is no time for anything more than determining what the problem is. Since the only safe place is on the surface, it boils down to one and only one action. The diver must immediately become buoyant and go directly to the surface.

When there is a single, simple procedure for an action, the diver will automatically follow that procedure. However, if there are multiple options, or the procedure is complicated, they may fail. All the agencies have contingency procedures. The key is to repeat the proper procedure over and over until it becomes an automatic, conditioned response.

■ *THE EXCEPTION TO THE RULE.* There is at least one glaring exception to the above statement, concerning the sudden onset of sickness.

If a diver becomes nauseous while diving and actually vomits, they will probably be fine if they can just keep their wits about them. They simply vomit and then replace their regulator, clear it and begin breathing again. However, vomit hitting the larynx sometimes causes it to tighten, which results in what is known as a *laryngeal spasm*. These spasms can also result from the sudden introduction of cold salt water against the larynx.

When a spasm occurs, the person can't inhale or exhale for a moment, and sometimes for more than a moment. In time the larynx will relax and allow breathing to resume, but if the diver panics and does what seems like the natural thing and heads for the surface, the probability of an embolism is almost certain. This is one instance where the diver *must* override their natural inclination to shoot to the surface and just stop, relax, and wait for the spasm to go away.

There is no way I know of to adequately prepare a person for the sudden onset of sickness beyond making them aware of its possibility and giving them a careful explanation of how to remain calm and not panic. Most will respond. They are the ones who will stand and fight. Some won't; they will turn and run at the first sign of trouble. They're the ones whose survival instincts overrule their thought process. For these people there is always going to be the potential for trouble under water.

Perhaps someday there will be a way to identify those individuals who are prone to panic and find some special way to prepare them for the unexpected situations. Until that time, you must do everything that you as an instructor can do to teach your students to relax, remain calm, and determine what the problem is before they react.

■ *SUMMARY.* If the diver is going to be prepared for contingencies, they must know what kind of problems are likely to develop and know how to react. You can teach them how to determine immediately if a problem is one they can work through (solvable), or one which they must deal with right now (unsolvable). Whichever problem they may have, they must always remain calm and let their training guide them.

Viable and Non-viable Options

When you are training a diver to get out of trouble, they first need to identify what the problem is. We just covered that. As their instructor, you need to know how they may react once they become aware that they are in trouble (the psycho-respiratory cycle), and then what will and won't work to get them out of trouble (viable and nonviable options).

The student isn't going to take the time to sort through all the things we've talked about so far, and they certainly aren't going to stop and consider why or how they got into trouble while they run through the options they've been taught for saving their lives. Instead, they are relying on you to understand all these things and to teach them a simple, reliable procedure for dealing with trouble if it arises. If I can help you understand the whole process, maybe you can do the same for them.

PSYCHO-RESPIRATORY CYCLE

Several times earlier in the book I referred to the psycho-respiratory cycle. I noted that it isn't something that the diver wants to get started because of where it could lead. I also said that when they are stressed they start to breathe faster, which raises their anxiety level, which makes them breathe even faster, and so on.

The actual process is somewhat more involved, and the results are at least predictable if not absolutely certain. So let's take a more detailed look at just what it is and how it works. To understand how it works you need to know:

- WHAT THE CYCLE IS
- HOW THE CYCLE BEGINS
- THE RESULTS OF THE CYCLE

To see clearly what the cycle is you almost have to start at the end. That is, you need to know what the possible result of the cycle is to fully grasp why it is so potentially dangerous.

The end result of the cycle is panic, which is defined as *a sudden overpowering fear*. A fear so strong that the will to survive completely takes over and all rational thought process just disappears. As I mentioned before, when that happens the results can be bad, even deadly.

Fortunately, the cycle can be broken at any time. There is absolutely no reason why a diver should ever be overcome by panic once they understand just what is happening to them.

■ *WHAT THE HECK IS A PSYCHO-RESPIRATORY CYCLE?* It's what every person who experiences panic goes through leading up to the panic attack. The good news is that the onset of the cycle doesn't have to end in panic, if the person is aware that it is happening and knows how to stop it.

It all begins with some kind of triggering mechanism, something called a *stressor*. It can be almost anything, but usually the source is very subtle. Typically, the individual would have prior outside stress before the dive. Tired, upset, not feeling just right, maybe out of sorts from traffic on the way to the dive site, but whatever it is, it already exists when they actually start getting ready for the dive. Then, during the getting ready stage, maybe some little thing doesn't go the way it should. Like the O-ring is missing on the tank valve or they forgot one of their gloves, or any of a number of things you could name—it doesn't take much. By the time they are ready to get into the water they are a little more on edge, and just slightly more stressed out.

This is the time they should stop and relax and let the stress go, because from this point on there is a good chance for everything to start snow-balling.

■ *AND SO THE CYCLE BEGINS.* Once in the water, perhaps the diver's buoyancy isn't quite right and they fight to keep off the bottom or to stay under water. Or maybe their wet suit is too tight across the shoulders and it puts too much strain on their neck when they swim in a horizontal position. Regardless, it is something that they don't really perceive as a problem, and under normal circumstances it wouldn't be one. Whatever the stressor is, it begins to create a sense of anxiety, and once they begin to feel anxious they have actually entered the cycle. But, as I said earlier, if they just recognize what's happening, they can stop it, immediately!

Anxiety causes the diver's heart to beat faster and they begin to breathe a little harder. That causes their oxygen level to drop and their carbon dioxide level to rise. The increase in CO_2 and the loss of O_2 raises the anxiety level even further, as well as causing the diver to feel the need for additional air which makes them breathe even harder. As you can see, they are now deeply into the cycle, each problem feeding on the other and making them both worse.

■ *THE NEEDLESS RESULT.* Unless the cycle is interrupted, it will continue on to its obvious conclusion: panic! It will get to the point where everything seems out of control, and if anything happens to create some additional outside stress, like the appearance of a dangerous animal, the diver may go over the edge and lose all ability to think rationally. Unfortunately, it may not require an additional stressor; it is very possible that the cycle can continue on its own and just keep going until the person loses control.

The whole point is not to let things progress to the point where there is a potential for trouble. If the diver learns to recognize the onset of the cycle, they can simply choose not to let it continue. It is up to you as the instructor to teach them how to recognize the problem and make it okay for them to just stop and regroup, or even abort the dive altogether.

VIABLE OPTIONS

A viable option is one that works! You know, sometimes I scare myself with these kind of profound statements. Obviously, it has to work to be viable. But ever since the beginning of scuba instruction there have been exercises or procedures taught that were presented in the name of equipment handling or dexterity skills, that had the tendency to confuse the diver under stress and may actually have contributed to the problem. So my rule is that anything taught in a scuba class has to meet two very strict criteria:

- WILL IT WORK UNDER THE WORST POSSIBLE CONDITIONS?
- IS THE PROCEDURE A FUNCTION OF AN ACTUAL DIVING SITUATION?

■ *WHAT ARE VIABLE OPTIONS?* You want to teach only the things that work. Why would you ever show a student a method, procedure, or exercise—whatever you want to call it—that could possibly confuse them under stress? The whole idea is to remove the confusion and teach them to react correctly the first time, every time.

A classic example of a viable option that works every time is the emergency buoyant ascent. This skill was originally developed by Ed Brawley and Jean Gregor. It was based on the reasonable assumption that if you have nothing to breathe and no one to help you, your only option is to go to the surface and get some air.

It would logically follow that if you are going to start for the surface, you should do whatever you can to make sure you get there. Not only that, but if you should pass out on the way up, there should be a way to make sure you stay there and not slip back under the water.

Before I explain how this works, let me say a word about this skill. It has been controversial over the years because of the way it was originally taught. In the original version, the diver's air was turned off and left off until they reached the surface. The fear was that the student would panic and, having nothing to breathe, would somehow get into trouble. To my knowledge this never happened, but as you will see, some changes were made based on input from diving physiologists from around the world who gathered at a seminar sponsored by the Underwater Medical Society. I am personally aware of *many millions* of these ascents having been done by students since 1968 *without incident*. Unfortunately, it is impossible to account for how many people have saved themselves because they had a method for doing so.

In a real out-of-air situation, the first thing the diver notices is that it becomes harder to breathe, and within a very few breaths, the air flow stops altogether. At that point, the diver wants to establish instant dependable buoyancy so they are assured of getting to the surface and staying there.

In the exercise, the out-of-air situation is simulated by the instructor turning off the student's air. The instructor keeps hold of the students tank valve and watches carefully to ensure the student is all right. If anything looks wrong, the air is turned back on immediately. Once the student realizes they are out of air, they reach down and locate their weight system, then carefully and deliberately remove the weights and place them out away from their body to ensure they are not going to get caught up on other equipment. As soon as the student begins to remove their weight belt, the instructor turns their air back on so they can resume breathing at any time should it become necessary.

As soon as the weights are gone, they look up and then start for the surface, making sure they allow air to escape from their mouth as they ascend. The regulator remains in the mouth, as there is always the possibility that in a real emergency the air supply will expand during ascent and offer them some additional breaths. They should also keep their hand on their exhaust valve during ascent so they can release excess air if they become too buoyant.

Once they reach the surface, they can add more air to their BC to make themselves more buoyant, but the lack of a weight belt will give them more than enough buoyancy to ensure they remain on the surface.

There are two things that are critical to the success of this exercise. One is that there are no options, and the second is that the student performs a deliberate act in the form of placing the belt away from their body. The first removes confusion, and the second focuses their mind and keeps them from rushing too fast and doing something wrong.

■ *THE OPTION SORTING PROCESS.* The human mind is like a computer: You put information into a computer to use at a later date, and when asked the right question, the computer will sort through the information in its memory and give the best answer or answers it can provide. The mind does essentially the same thing: It sorts through everything it knows and then tells the body what to do. The problem is, when a diver is under stress the mind won't search all the options. It will just go to the first one that has made a big impression on the memory, and that's what it will tell the body to do.

■ *SELECTING THE ONE THAT WORKS.* As you can imagine, if the decision is the wrong one, the body does the wrong thing and there is the possibility of an accident. On the other hand, if there is only one option, one skill that is imprinted on the diver's brain, they will do the one right thing the first time, every time.

■ *A CONDITIONED AUTOMATIC RESPONSE* is your goal and the answer to the problem of reacting to a panic situation. In order to develop an automatic response you must:

- IDENTIFY THE PROBLEM
- DETERMINE A REACTION THAT WORKS, EVERY TIME
- ELIMINATE ANY OTHER CHOICES
- PRACTICE THE RESPONSE UNTIL CONDITIONED TO DO IT AUTOMATICALLY

It should be abundantly clear by now why it is so important to simplify contingency skills, and then to practice them over and over until they become completely automatic, conditioned responses. The only skills you want to teach are viable skills that work every time under the worst conditions. Never teach a so-called skill that has the potential to become a problem.

NON-VIABLE OPTIONS

Non-viable options are ones that won't work under the worst conditions. It may seem a little redundant to say that again, but like much of what we have covered, it bears repeating. The principle reasons that non-viable options don't work is they are too complicated, they can't be sustained, and they lead to unforeseen trouble.

A non-viable option doesn't always have to be just a contingency skill either. It can be a simple everyday action that becomes a bad habit which under rough conditions can mean trouble.

■ *IT JUST WON'T WORK* when the conditions reach their worst. These are the little things that a student must learn in order to dive safely. They shouldn't have to learn the hard way that diving is made up of lots of little things that come together to form the activity. One example of a little thing that doesn't work under the worst possible conditions, and which if allowed to become a bad habit could lead to trouble, is putting the mask up on the forehead.

This doesn't seem like that big of a deal, but when a diver gets in the habit of coming to the surface and putting their mask up on their forehead, they risk the very real possibility of losing it in heavy water. Or it could be another diver simply knocking it off. In any event, if it happens and the mask is lost, the diver could end up in trouble since one of their best protections on the surface is to keep the water out of their eyes and be able to maintain their vision. It's also pretty nice not to have water running up your nose. What should be done is to put the mask down around the neck. That way, if the water gets rough they simply put it back on, and they don't need to worry about it being knocked off either.

I mentioned earlier about the problem of swimming on the back: how it can wear out your upper front leg muscles, which means you are pretty much done swimming. As long as the diver swims face-down, they can keep on going for much longer, even if they get tired.

This lesson was learned the hard way by two old diving buddies of mine. They went on a night dive only to surface and discover they were in the middle of a huge storm. The wind and current took them down the middle of a very long lake. One of the two (who, by the way, were brothers) lost his snorkel and couldn't swim face-down very well, so he swam on his back. Eventually his upper legs cramped and he was unable to swim at all. Fortunately, his brother stayed on his stomach and was able to tow him until his legs were rested enough to swim again. Since that time I have witnessed several other incidents that have made me a firm believer in only swimming face-down.

These are just two examples of how small, non-viable options to a diving technique can become a problem. Think every action through and be sure that you don't teach your student a way to get hurt.

■ *TOO MANY OPTIONS* may be the biggest contributor to accidents that result from diver panic. While I think it should now be quite clear what is meant by too many options, let me give you an idea how it can manifest itself and how well-intended training exercises can actually contribute to the problem.

This example is about an exercise that was used for many years as an equipment handling drill. I'm talking about the old *ditch and recovery*. In this drill the diver was taught to remove their equipment on the bottom and then ascend to the surface. They would then return to the bottom, assemble the equipment and put it back on. There is no doubt that the student developed their equipment handling skills, but under stress it had the potential for setting up an accident. Actually, I never did understand the purpose of this drill. I know of no real-life diving situation where a diver would want to remove their equipment, go to the surface, and then go back and get it. For that matter, have you ever heard of anyone ever throwing their equipment overboard and then going to the bottom and putting it on? If you have, try to avoid ever getting that person as a buddy.

There have been a large number of diving accidents over the years where the victim was found on the bottom with air in their tank and a functioning regulator. For some reason, in many of these cases the victim attempted to remove their tank from their shoulders, but not the waist strap or the weight belt. So they were found with the tank hanging from their waist, weight belt still on, and plenty of air in a delivery system that worked fine.

I'm not sure what this scene conveys to you, but my opinion is that they had a problem and became frightened. Because they had been taught to remove their equipment, they somehow drew a connection between getting rid of their equipment and getting to the surface, even though they weren't taught to remove it under those conditions. They just did the first thing that entered their mind. They tore off the shoulder straps—but by that time they were out of breath and didn't get the rest of the job done. The problem was that panic prevented them from thinking it through, and they couldn't complete the process so they died.

The point here is that no matter how well-intended, the exercise they were taught wasn't representative of a real diving situation. What's more, in my opinion it actually impacted the end result, because it was only one of several so-called life-saving techniques that not only didn't save their life, but quite possibly contributed to their death. That, my friends, is the ultimate non-viable option.

■ *SUMMARY.* As in the previous chapters, there has been a common thread weaving its way through the verbiage here. I spoke of how to make a decision about what kind of a problem existed, and what to do when that decision was made.

There are really only two kinds of problems: the ones you have time to solve, and the ones that you have to do something about *right now*. The only thing the diver needs to decide is, does he or she have time to fix the problem, or do they need to react immediately. The solvable problems aren't the big concern since they can be solved. It's the ones that we have to react to—or maybe die as a result of—that seem to demand our attention.

The common thread has to do with how you prepare for, recognize, and react to a life-threatening situation. The answer is a short one. You have one and only one response to any given problem. There can be no confusing options. When you have nothing to breathe and your life is in danger, you go to the surface and get some air. The procedure must be practiced until it becomes a *completely automatic, conditioned response.* That is the key! Teach your students to remain calm, decide what the problem is, and then react quickly in the right way. When in doubt, err on the side of safety. You never make a mistake by saving your life.

CHAPTER 4

When to Pass– And When Not To

Knowing when to pass a student and when not to is possibly the most critical ability you need to develop as an instructor. It's important to *you* because you may have to tell a paying customer that they spent their money and didn't make it. But, it's *very* important to the *student*, not only because they spent the money, but because their life may depend on your decision.

There is a great deal more involved in deciding when to pass a person than whether or not the student is happy. The bottom line is that, for lots of reasons, you simply cannot pass a person who isn't ready. So the real challenge becomes how you tell them they aren't going to pass and still keep them in the program and as a customer. It is the single most difficult thing you will do as an instructor—and can require some top notch diplomacy. In fact, it puts me in mind of the old saying, "you need to be able to tell a person to go to hell and make 'em look forward to the trip." That's not what you're doing, but it sort of feels that way when *you* have to do it.

The truth is, not passing someone who isn't ready is good for both parties if it is handled right. In this chapter I'll cover a whole bunch of reasons why passing someone who isn't ready is bad for you and them. Once you understand the reasons why, we'll examine how to determine when they *are* ready, and I'll give you some hard criteria for making the decision. Finally, I'll show you some ways to salvage the situation, keep the customer, and hopefully at some point, make them a diver.

You are going to find that most of the people who have problems in class either lack the proper motivation or are afraid. I think you will find that woven in among the various ideas are guidelines for helping the student overcome their fear and giving them the proper motivation, and in most cases, a deep desire to not only complete the course, but to do so in a highly successful manner.

Why Passing a Student Who Isn't Ready is Bad for You Both

The first thing that needs to be absolutely clear is that *there is no up side* to passing a student who isn't ready. I'm going to make a list here of all the things I can think of that are bad, but there is no list of good things—not even one. So let's take a look at the two sides of the story. First, the reasons why it is bad for the student, and then we'll look at why it's just as bad for the instructor.

HOW IT HURTS THE STUDENT

■ *EVERYONE'S AT RISK* even though the first consideration—and the most obvious one—is the diver's safety.

When you send a person out on their own with a certification card, the diving operator to whom they eventually go for air or equipment probably won't know their actual qualifications. The operator will logically assume that since the person has a card that says they are qualified to go diving, they are, in fact, qualified. The dive operator will then provide them with whatever they need, and in many cases send them out on their charter boat to a dive site that may be beyond the diver's abilities. Since that person wasn't ready to go diving in the first place, you can imagine the potential for trouble if they go on a really difficult dive.

Not only does this put the individual at risk, but there is a significant and unwarranted burden placed on the dive operator. The probability is that if a certified diver has an accident while diving from a charter boat, the boat operator will be named as the responsible party first; the original instructor second. Unfortunately, they may also name the agency that produced the card when, in fact, the agency did nothing more than issue a certification on the instructor's behalf to an individual who they were assured was qualified. The agency didn't teach or test the person, but they have been put at risk as well, and for what?

■ *THEY WASTED THEIR TIME AND MONEY,* because in spite of what I said in the previous couple of paragraphs, most people who don't feel comfortable probably won't even make an attempt to go diving.

I find it particularly sad when I think of a person spending their hard earned money to learn how to participate in a sport they have been dreaming about—some for their entire life—and when they finally take the opportunity to learn how to dive, they don't quite get it done. They don't actually fail, but they fall short of their expectations and what they wanted to accomplish. They don't feel comfortable in the water and they understand instinctively that they're at risk, so they don't follow through. They just give up! As far as the *student* is concerned, they've just wasted their time and money, but if you ask me, it's *the instructor* who's wasted the student's time and money: the instructor had control and let them down. This may not be true in every case, but it is in far too many. However, that's another story and will be covered later. Let's move on.

■ *IT'S JUST ANOTHER BAD EXPERIENCE* in a long line of bad experiences in today's world.

It seems to me that everywhere you turn, whether you are seeking a service or a product, it is almost routine that the provider falls short of their promises and doesn't satisfactorily complete the job for which they were paid.

To me this is a very sorry commentary on what is happening in society. It seems that many people have come to believe it is acceptable to promise a specific performance, be paid a fair price for it, and then, in return, give the customer far less than what they paid for and had a right to expect.

Experience has taught me that if we as instructors give people everything they paid for, we can expect that the return will be satisfied customers. What's more, they'll tell everyone they meet that you can be depended upon to do what you promised. That's not only the right and fair thing, it's what you would and should expect in their place.

■ **SUMMARY.** As I said earlier, there are no up sides for the student who is passed when not ready. They always lose! But they aren't the only ones who suffer. The instructor, the dive store, and the industry at large all stand to lose every bit as much as the student does, at least in terms of time and money.

HOW IT HURTS THE INSTRUCTOR

When you make the decision to pass a student who might not be quite ready, you truly do them a disservice, even if they never put their own safety at risk. In addition, you stand to do yourself a good deal of harm. The greatest concern is always for the *well-being* of the student, but if they aren't also *happy*, they can make your business life miserable.

■ **THE BEST PART OF A BAD SITUATION,** and the most you can hope for as an instructor, is that the student who is passed prematurely is somehow satisfied enough with having actually completed the class—so much so that they don't really mind if they never go diving. This happens!

Maybe it's because the student is too embarrassed to complain, or they think it is their own fault they aren't comfortable enough to go diving. Whatever it is, this particular type of individual probably won't say anything negative to other people. I can assure you however, that these people are more the exception than the rule. The rest are among the most talkative people in the world.

The dissatisfied, vocal person is your worst public relations nightmare. They will tell everyone who will listen, at every conceivable opportunity, how terrible diving is, how you were a horrid instructor, and that anyone who takes up scuba diving is a fool. If these people are well respected in normal life, they can have a profoundly negative impact on your reputation and financial future.

For some reason, the dissatisfied seem to talk more and be more persuasive than the satisfied; it's just one of the great mysteries of life.

■ *THEY AREN'T BUYERS, THEY ARE SELLERS,* and that can hit you in the pocketbook twice.

The greatest percentage of dissatisfied students won't ever buy any equipment. At least not beyond the basic mask, snorkel, and fins. They hit you in the pocketbook once because they represent a lost sale. If they had been happy with their abilities and felt comfortable going diving, they probably would have bought at least the basic scuba gear.

There is another group that get excited initially, and before they even finish the course, they buy everything they can get their hands on and will fit on their credit card.

These people are almost worse than the ones who don't buy in the first place. Why? Because at some point they are going to dump their equipment on the open market. That's a potential problem from two points of view.

First, the person who buys the equipment may or may not be a certified diver that is qualified to use the equipment and able to determine whether it functions as it should.

Second, it takes a sale away from the dive store. Sure, the dive store made the initial sale, but had the person who originally bought it been happy, they would have kept their equipment, and the person who bought it later would have then been a new customer for the dive store.

The instructor must never lose sight of the fact that one of the main reasons scuba training is offered is to create customers who will buy equipment. That fact does not represent a contradiction to training the best divers the instructor can possibly produce. In fact, as you may have already surmised, the only people who will buy the equipment and actually go use it are the ones who are properly trained and feel confident about their abilities.

For some reason, there are still instructors who feel reluctant to sell or even suggest that a student buy equipment. I have always found this attitude fascinating. *YOU CAN'T GO DIVING WITHOUT EQUIPMENT!* Who is the most trusted source of information on all things about diving? *THE INSTRUCTOR!* This whole thing shouldn't be a big mystery. Who else are they going to turn to? It is not only okay for the instructor to guide their equipment decisions; it is logical, and in my mind, it's the right thing to do.

■ *SUMMARY.* These then are the principle reasons that a student should never be passed until they are ready:

- It hurts the student by putting them at risk (not to mention the risk for the instructor), it wastes their time and money because they probably will never attempt to go diving if they don't feel comfortable in the water, and it is just one more bad experience with another jerk who promised something they couldn't or wouldn't deliver.

  From my point of view, none of these is acceptable, but the instructor has absolute control over making sure they deliver what they promised, so there is simply no excuse for doing less.

- It also hurts the instructor because the unhappy student will tell everyone they meet never to try scuba, or that if they do, to at least make sure they don't go to you for the instruction.

- They rarely buy anything, but if they do, they turn right around and dump it on the open market, possibly to an unqualified buyer. Plus, they ruin the probability of another sale for the store.

All in all, it seems pretty clear to me that nobody wins in any of the above scenarios. In fact, everyone loses, and I simply don't believe that it's necessary for *anyone* to lose. All that needs to be done is to make sure that before anyone receives a certification card they are *ready*. As you will see later in this chapter, for those who aren't ready, make sure you give them every opportunity to succeed, and they will make every effort to do so.

Not Passing the Unpassable

At certification time, students tend to fall into one of three categories:

- They are obviously qualified and ready to go diving on their own.
- They are just as obviously *not* qualified and are completely aware of that fact.
- They are in that gray area where they have technically met all the standard requirements, but just barely. They passed the written tests, so as far as the ordinary instructor is concerned, the student is ready to be certified since they met the letter of the certifying agency's requirements.

However, for the best instructors, there is still doubt about this last type of person. They haven't yet seen that elusive something that tells them deep down in their gut that this student is *ready*.

The question is, how do you decide what to do when all the measurable criteria that can possibly be devised by your certification agency have been met by the student, yet as the instructor you *still* have reservations?

That kind of situation requires a subjective decision, and until now there hasn't been any objective way to help you make it. Having said that, it should be noted that the best instructors do use objective criteria to make their decisions, but they are rarely, if ever, aware of it. They just seem to know intuitively what to do. They may or may not give the right reasons to the student, but they will do the right thing even if they couldn't tell you the exact reasons why.

What I want to do here is to help provide the means for making the tough decisions. I want to offer you what I choose to call *semi-objective* criteria for deciding when that gray-area student is ready.

You might wonder why I call it semi-objective criteria, since almost by definition it is either objective or it isn't. As you will see, there is no way to apply measurable numbers to the personal evaluation process, so that you are able to say for sure that a student is 95% perfect. And since it only requires 90% to pass, they must be ready. But what you can do to make the decision more objective is ask yourself the right questions—questions that can be answered yes or no about the *way* the student performed the skills.

The proper time to certify the student is when all the questions can be answered *yes*! This is not a method that offers measurable numbers to make it totally objective, but it is one that gives you clear criteria that requires specific answers. Answers that can help you make your decision. Hence the term *semi-objective criteria*. It works for me, and I believe it will for you.

In this chapter, we will cover four primary areas of interest:

- SEMI-OBJECTIVE CRITERIA
- TURNING THE NON-PASSER INTO A DIVER
- HOW TO TAKE ON THE "PROJECT"
- ISSUING THE CHALLENGE

First I'll show you how to decide for sure when a student *isn't* ready to be certified. Then I'll tell you how to save them as a customer and turn them into the kind of diver you want them to be. Easy to say, but not always so easy to do—although it's not nearly as difficult as you might imagine.

SEMI-OBJECTIVE CRITERIA

Before we can talk about the specifics of the criteria for deciding if a student should be certified, you must first have a clearer understanding of some of the terms I use to describe the student's readiness for certification. I'm concerned that unless you understand exactly what I'm talking about, there may be some confusion when it comes to explaining the criteria.

There are several terms I have used throughout the book to indicate the student's readiness for certification. They are:

- BEING "COMFORTABLE"
- DOING IT "RIGHT"
- BEING "READY"

■ *BEING COMFORTABLE* means simply that! The student is in every way comfortable with what they are doing. They are relaxed, unhurried, and confident in their ability. They are so sure they can perform the skill properly that they typically demonstrate it *overly* slow just to emphasize to the instructor how totally relaxed and capable they are. I've heard instructors describe these students as looking almost bored with the exercise and ready to get on with something else.

■ *DOING IT "RIGHT"* is of course the only way to do something. But the issue here is the application of the term to the student's demonstration of their skills.

Certification agencies, individually and as a group, do everything possible to establish measurable standards of performance that their combined years of research have shown to be the essential qualifications the student must possess in order to receive certification.

The problem with the written criteria is that there is a human factor that must also be evaluated, and it simply isn't measurable in numeric terms. This part of the evaluation involves an attitude, a look, a feeling that the student emits that tells the instructor the student has met more than the letter of the requirements, they have also met the intent. This kind of evaluation can only be made by another human being who is capable of recognizing the signs.

When a student isn't quite comfortable with a skill, they tend to rush. They are usually tense, and often there is a noticeable hesitation before they attempt a skill. Sometimes they are concerned about the difficulty of the skill, or maybe they're just unsure of how or what to do. But they are almost always stiff, hesitant to start, and in a hurry to get it over with.

Doing it right means they are relaxed, unhurried, and perform the skill calmly. If they are comfortable with their ability they don't get excited if they don't get their mask completely cleared on the first attempt. They just take another breath and finish the job. They know the goal isn't being able to clear the mask on the first breath— the goal is to get it clear without feeling hurried or anxious.

■ *BEING "READY"* for certification is the culmination of all their training and is also the ultimate question the instructor must answer before issuing the student their card. But what is ready?

Clearly the student has to do everything "right," and they must be "comfortable" with their skills, but there is something more. Being ready means they are prepared to go diving with a buddy, and without professional supervision. It means that their buddy can depend on them just as they can depend on their buddy.

There are a series of questions that you must ask yourself about each student before you issue their card. These are the semi-objective criteria that must be met in order for them to be certified. The questions are objective in the sense that you must be able to answer yes to every question before you pass them. But they are still somewhat subjective in that they lack numeric quantification, and in order to be answered at all, require careful observation skills on the part of the instructor.

THE QUESTIONS!

■ *ARE THEY REALLY COMFORTABLE IN THE WATER?* There are lots of signs that tell you when a person isn't comfortable in the water. They struggle to stay on the surface, they attempt to breathe around their mouthpiece as though they can't get enough air from their snorkel or regulator, and several other things I covered earlier.

When they are comfortable, *they'll look* like *you feel* in the water. They'll be relaxed at everything they do. Almost like they would rather be in the water than anywhere else, and could stay there forever.

■ *ARE THEY REALLY COMFORTABLE WITH THE SKILLS?* This question is actually made up of several sub-questions that, when combined, will give you the answer to the main question. The sub-questions which I feel provide the keys to determining the student's comfort level are:

• Do they assemble their equipment and get dressed efficiently? Just like I said before, if they hesitate, forget things, can't remember exactly how to assemble the equipment even though they have been doing it for several classes, and so forth, they aren't comfortable. They should be eager and well organized. Dressing should be quick and efficient and regarded as nothing more than the bothersome thing you do (*without effort*) before you get in the water.

- Do they make sure that everything is properly adjusted before they enter the water? This is another key—it tells you a great deal about how comfortable they are with both their equipment and their skill level.

  A good diver wants to feel "together." By this I mean they want everything to feel like a unit, not a series of disconnected pieces of equipment hanging from their body. When they *aren't* comfortable, they tend to forget to make sure everything is as it should be.

- Can they clear their mask in a relaxed, confident manner? Mask clearing is a special indicator that tells you volumes about their overall comfort level. If they can clear their mask and it's no big deal, the chances are excellent they can do the other skills just as well.

- Is buoyancy control second nature? Like the mask clearing, if they can maintain neutral buoyancy without really thinking about it, they're getting pretty darned comfortable.

■ *ARE THEY READY TO BE A BUDDY YOU COULD DEPEND ON?* Instructors get so accustomed to students depending on them, that often they forget that in a buddy team, they each must be able to depend on the other. A real good test of the student's readiness is whether the instructor would want them as a buddy and feels they could be depended upon if the need should arise.

■ *IF THE STUDENT WAS YOUR SON OR DAUGHTER, WOULD YOU WANT THEM TO GO DIVING WITHOUT PROFESSIONAL SUPERVISION?* For me, this is the ultimate question, and the one which supercedes all others.

This question became important to me when my son, who was 13 years old at the time, asked if he could work for the summer at a resort store I owned. It meant that for the first time he would be diving without my care and custody.

He had been diving since he was 6 years old, and by the time he was 13 he had about 200 hours of *night diving* under his belt. Still, I was a concerned father who wanted to make sure his son was ready to go diving with someone else.

For the first time since I had been teaching scuba diving, I suddenly realized that *everyone* is someone's son, daughter, wife, husband, or whatever—and each and every one of them deserves the same kind of concern that I had for my son.

All this might seem a little obvious, but for me, students had always been informed adults making adult decisions about their own lives. I had always cared and tried to do the best job I knew how, but when it concerned my own son it put things into a whole new perspective. From that point on, I have always asked that question last—even when all the other questions have been answered yes, I still ask myself if I would let them go if they were my loved one.

Just so you know and I don't leave you wondering, I did let my son go that summer, and he was ready!

■ *SUMMARY.* There are a few simple questions you need to ask yourself which must be answered *yes* before you give a student their certification. The questions cover the sense of the student's performance more than the letter of the requirements.

If you are able to answer yes to the questions, without exception, you can say with confidence that the student is ready.

Keep the Non-Passer as a Customer and Turn Them Into a Diver

THE STUDENT "KNOWS"

Don't ever kid yourself about the student's sense of how they are doing. It would be a rare person who doesn't make constant comparisons between themselves and the other students. They are always aware of where they stand. So when it comes time to tell them they aren't ready to be certified, why do some students make such a big fuss about it? And why are instructors as a group so terror-stricken at the prospect of having to tell them?

Just like everything else to this point, there are no *simple* answers. That's the bad news! The good news is that there *are* answers. Let's take a look at the different attitudes you are liable to encounter from the student, and how you deal with each one.

■ *NO MATTER HOW MUCH THEY PROTEST,* they already know! In fact, the students that cry the loudest are generally the ones who are most aware of their own shortcomings.

Their protest is typically nothing more than a face-saving gesture, which in their mind shifts the blame from themselves to the instructor, and allows them to keep their self-esteem. Either that, or they are just big babies and can't take responsibility for their own failures. Whichever way it is, their nature demands that they protest before they accept the outcome.

Once the student is over the protest stage, one of two things will happen. Either they will accept the fact and then do what is needed to correct the problem, or their pride will force them to a state of indignation that demands they stomp away in fury. The instructor's job is to prevent the stomping part and to deal with them in a way that keeps their indignation from getting too strong.

The best way to deal with this personality type is to never let it be *their* fault to begin with. Let's face it, if an instructor walked up to you and said "you fail," a little righteous indignation would probably be in order. On the other hand, if you, as the instructor, would say,

"I feel like I let you down somewhere during the class, and I just don't think it would be fair to you to send you out diving until you had the chance to really get comfortable." By doing this you have relieved the student of responsibility. It's your fault, not theirs, and you're just giving them what they paid for. It isn't a punishment or a failure of any kind, so they aren't threatened, they are relieved. You gave them an out and let them save face. Not only are they now unlikely to quit, but they should have the resolve and the attitude needed to stay with it until they get it right.

■ *NOT PASSING IS SPELLED R-E-L-I-E-F,* and that is exactly what most unpassable students feel when they find out they don't have to get certified. I know that sounds funny—to say they don't *have* to get certified—but the truth, as I just mentioned above, is that most people sense how they are doing, and they are especially aware if they don't feel all that good about their comfort level with diving.

The attitude problems for students who don't pass usually develop because they have too much pride to admit they aren't ready, either to the instructor or even to themselves. It's also possible that they aren't able to judge how the other students feel (even though they can see how they look), and as a result, they may think the other students feel just like they do, and since the other students seem anxious to get certified, maybe they're ready too.

The technique for talking to these people is much the same as for the loud protester. There isn't any difference in the way they feel about their skills, the difference is in how they react to the fact that they won't be certified.

I don't know of any way to accurately predict whether the non-passer will protest or be openly relieved. What I do know is that if you take the approach that it's your problem and not theirs, you will most likely make a fast friend of that person. Whether they yell and complain or show open relief, no one wants to be made to feel like a failure! When a student shows relief, it is simply a reaction to the fact that they no longer have to fear doing something they *know* they aren't ready for and which may, in fact, put their lives at risk.

I don't mean to give the impression that everything has to be someone's fault. In fact, whenever possible, the attitude you want to establish is that the student is never judged on being good or bad. There shouldn't be any hint of a pass/fail mentality at all. Instead, the students should understand they are being evaluated based on whether they are *ready* or they *aren't*. They must believe there are no failures in your course, only some who are ready sooner than others.

The attitude you want to convey to your students is "you did that well, but I know you can do better. Let's work on it a little more and get it perfect." Or, it might be, "wow, you're really getting good. You've come a long way since you started. It won't be long now until you'll have it nailed."

What you want to accomplish is for them to feel successful at everything they do. You encourage continued effort by making them clearly aware that you believe they have done well to this point and are destined to be excellent divers, even if it takes them a little longer.

■ *KEEP THEM AS CUSTOMERS* by making them good divers. All of the suggestions and techniques I have been talking about boil down to one thing. Never, never, never, never, give up on a student! Do everything you can dream of to keep them in class and working to become a diver. If you do, good things will happen. They'll tell everyone what a great instructor you are, they'll want to go diving, and since they can't go diving without equipment they will also be customers. In fact, after the care and consideration you have shown, they wouldn't dream of going anywhere else to buy.

You probably expected a long philosophic dissertation on how to keep the student as a customer. Sorry! It just isn't that complicated. Simply take care of the customer, and they'll take care of you.

Take on the "Project"

We've covered in a general way how to keep the student as a customer and make them a diver. What we haven't done is explore the nitty-gritty of getting the job done.

Very early on in this book I mentioned that the real reward in diving instruction came from taking the student who "just couldn't do it," and turning them into a competent diver. It's as true now as it was way back then. But, if you're going to climb that hill, there are several things you have to do first. They are:

- LOSE YOUR EGO
- BECOME A PSYCHOLOGIST
- MAKE THE STUDENT SPECIAL
- DO WHAT IS NEEDED

LOSE YOUR EGO

In order for the instructor to help the problem student, they must first climb down off their pedestal. By that I mean you must be willing to humble yourself in front of the student and possibly the whole class. It may also be necessary to accept responsibility for things that aren't your fault. To do that you have to lose your ego and get your reward from having accomplished a job that a lesser person couldn't have.

It seems to me that it is just human nature to not want to be wrong about or a failure at anything. Happily, some people possess that wonderful quality of never feeling threatened by criticism, and can accept it as a means to improve themselves. Others, and I think this is true of most people, feel judged and resent the criticism; they tend to react negatively when they receive it and to resent the giver as well.

What I'm trying to say is, never be judgmental in your teaching. Instead, when a student doesn't "get it," assume the reason they don't get it is because *you* didn't explain the process well enough for them to understand what to do. Let it be your problem, not theirs.

When you become judgmental, you may be right in your judgment, but you will also lose the student. You must choose whether you want to be a great teacher, or if your ego demands that you always be right.

BECOME A PSYCHOLOGIST

You might be getting the impression here that all the problems with students are simple and can be answered just as simply by the instructor being the fall guy. Not so! While it's true that humility is a great first step, there are lots of different problems that affect students and keep them from succeeding. If you are going to be successful as an instructor and help them become quality divers, you have to be able to look past their surface problems and dig out whatever is *truly* bothering them so you can correct the *real* problem.

Before someone—especially the presiding medical authority— starts worrying about instructors practicing medicine without a license, let me state clearly that no such thing is intended. Let's face it, even the trained professionals seem to be limited in their ability to understand their patients' problems and offer any certain course of recovery. So it only stands to reason that a scuba instructor, no matter how highly trained, is unlikely to actually get inside a student's head. They certainly aren't going to attempt any kind of treatment!

Having said all that, what the instructor can do, based on experience and observation, is to make an effort to look past surface explanations their students offer and attempt to better understand the real problem. Then, if it is within their power, help the student to understand how to solve the problem themselves.

It seems to me that in the very simplest terms, what a doctor tries to do is carefully guide the patient to an understanding of their own problems; however, you certainly don't have to be a doctor to know that when people understand what their problems are, they are much better equipped to deal with them.

In scuba instruction you are much more effective as an instructor if you can help the student understand their problems first and then help them find the solution—as opposed to simply pointing out their faults and telling them to get it right or fail the course.

MAKE THE STUDENT SPECIAL

Making the student special is the creation of an attitude *from* the instructor *to* the student. It is nothing more than having the student believe in the deepest part of their heart and mind that you really care for them and want them to succeed.

There is some danger that a student may interpret special to mean inferior, and somehow feel they don't measure up. What you want to accomplish is exactly the opposite of that feeling. You want the student who needs more time and attention to feel they are special because you are willing to give them what they need without making them feel "slow."

DO WHAT IS NEEDED

If there was ever a catch-all phrase, "do what is needed" is one of the most applicable. To me it means exactly what it says. If you are going to be consistently successful as an instructor, there are going to be times when you have to just throw away the rules—in a manner of speaking—and do whatever it takes to get the job done.

You will find that there are times when people don't follow the script your certification agency has given you. Every single student is different, and just when you think you have teaching figured out, one of these utterly unique individuals will throw you a curve that there just isn't any pat answer for.

If you think your certification agency has all the answers, just look at how much instructional programs have changed over the years. It would be foolish to believe the programs won't continue to change in the future as our knowledge and experience grow.

I certainly don't want to convey the impression that the instructor should do whatever they want to. Far from it! The wealth of experience that has gone into the development of instructional programs by the various agencies is priceless. Their programs represent the collective knowledge of all the instructors that have gone before, and have been carefully designed to help overcome the problems that students traditionally seem to have. What is more, the detailed procedures eliminate the need for the instructors to constantly reinvent their own system.

Nevertheless, there are still going to be times when situations develop that aren't specifically covered by agency procedures. If this happens, it becomes necessary for the instructor to fall back on their training, experience, and good judgment to "do what is needed" and get the job done.

Issue the Challenge

The last part of my formula for keeping the student in class and as a customer involves making them part of the solution. That is, presenting them with challenges they can meet so that when they finally reach their goal they will have earned it—and done so in a way that makes the accomplishment that much sweeter.

No one appreciates anything they get for nothing, or at least not as much as something they *earn*. So the idea is to give the student and yourself meaningful goals that are both realistic and reachable. What you want to do is:

- MAKE THEM A PART OF THE PROJECT
- GIVE THEM MEANINGFUL GOALS
- CLIMB THE MOUNTAIN
- NEVER QUIT UNTIL THEY DO—AND NEVER LET THEM

MAKE THEM A PART OF THE PROJECT

We have already talked about how the instructor needs to assure the students that they haven't failed. They may even have to let the student feel like the instructor was more responsible than the student was for not being ready to be certified.

While the instructor's position is fairly clear, the student still needs to be motivated to get the job done. One excellent way of doing that is to challenge them to be better—better even than they thought they could be.

Part of the challenge for the instructor is to make the student feel like a partner in the process. Nobody wants to be thought of as a charity case! They will be much happier if they understand that you aren't giving them anything more than the opportunity to be successful. The attitude you want to establish is no more complicated than "you can do this if you want to. I'm happy to work with you for as long as it takes providing you are willing to put forth the effort—it's up to you!"

GIVE THEM MEANINGFUL GOALS

A meaningful goal for one person will be different for another. Everyone has their own hot button that motivates them to keep going. The trick is to figure out what that button is for each student.

A very typical situation occurs when a wife, girlfriend, child, or sibling is pressured into taking the course by the husband, etc. I don't mean to imply that only men put the pressure on. It is just that for some reason it is more common for males to apply pressure than for females to. It is certainly more usual for the parent to pressure the child than for the child to pressure the parent, although you frequently do have a parent in the class because the child begged them until they gave in. In any event, when people in this situation struggle, one of the best challenges you can offer them is to strive to be better than whoever pushed them to join the class in the first place.

If you say to these people, "if you are willing, I believe I can help you become a better diver than your . . . . . !" (Husband, boyfriend, father, or whatever.) They may not believe you at first, but if you can help them make enough recognizable progress to give them hope, you will have moved them in the right direction. Sometimes all that needs to be done is to get them over one hurdle they thought they couldn't make—like clearing the mask. If they had viewed that process as something they might never be able to do, and you can help them become really good at it, that may be enough to unlock the door to their being able to master all the other skills as well.

It is quite probable that what the student finds overwhelming is the idea of trying to learn "everything." It is much better to let them take on one challenge at a time, and not get bogged down by thinking in terms of the whole course.

The point is, find a goal that is important to them—one that they feel is attainable. Don't let them feel overwhelmed to the point where the process seems like too much to deal with. Little successes lead to bigger ones.

CLIMB THE MOUNTAIN

Everyone is capable of more than they think they are. It's just that they don't always get the chance to prove it. In the case of completing a scuba course, the instructor's job is to make it possible for the students to prove it to themselves.

The journey to completion is kind of like mountain climbers helping each other to the summit. One leads, the other follows, but they both share in the accomplishment. The chinese proverb says that the longest journey begins with the first step. So it is with teaching. If the students looks at the class as a mountain to be climbed, they may give up emotionally before they ever really get started. But if you take them one little step at a time, then before they realize it, they're at the top. That's one of the very best reasons why you try to make sure a student is comfortable with the simpler skills before they move on to the next, more difficult one. At the same time, don't lose track of the fact that the goal is for the student to know everything by the *end* of the course. As the instructor, you must know the difference between the skills that must be done correctly before they move on, and the ones that can be practiced and accomplished along the way.

Try to never forget the fact that you and the student are partners. Neither can be successful without the other, just like the mountain climbers.

NEVER LET 'EM QUIT

Finally, we're at the point where we separate the instructors who view the students as money in the short term, from the instructors who see instead the obligation of their commitment to the student, and understand instinctively that if they fulfill that commitment, the money will follow.

The principal questions that instructors always ask when I tell them to do whatever is needed time-wise to make the students successful is, "who's going to pay for the extra time? Do we charge them for it or are we expected to pick up the tab?" This is the point at which I generally hang my head and say, "if you have to ask—you just don't get it."

When a student walks in the door of a scuba store and asks, "can you teach me how to dive?" there are two things they really want to know. The first is the answer to the question they just asked, and the second is how much it will cost.

Assuming your answer to the question of whether you can teach them to dive is "yes," then once you have told them the price, you have made a commitment. You just said you could do it. You probably didn't say you were charging for a certain number of hours of instruction, or a predefined number of dives—*you said you could teach them to dive!*

They paid you their money and signed up based on the belief that you would do what you said. They have a right to expect nothing less than you promised. Regardless of how long it takes, and without additional money.

The short-sighted instructor is now saying, "That's stupid! My time is worth money and if the student isn't able to get it by the time everyone else does, they can pay extra or forget it." These people will lose the student, along with all potential future sales and every potential new student the old one comes in contact with.

The instructor with vision sees what must be done, and generally (not always of course, but generally) reaps the reward. The student is happy, they become a diver, they frequently buy equipment, and they always tell potential future divers where to go for their lessons.

Believe me, you can't buy that kind of advertising for any price, but more importantly you did what was right. You kept your word and fulfilled your commitment. Never lose sight of the fact that every successful business is based on two fundamental things: service and integrity. Without both a business may be successful for a while, but in the long run, whoever offers them both will eventually win.

So there it is. Never quit until they do—and never let them! Don't let a student give up on themselves. Scuba diving is something that virtually anyone can do on some level. Maybe they won't make 250-foot dives on some lost wreck, but they can do some kind of diving, and it's all fun. Stay with them and trust in the knowledge that when you treat them right, somewhere, *somehow* you will be rewarded.

■ *SUMMARY.* When you pass a person who isn't "ready" it hurts you both. Nobody wins that one! They aren't a diver, or a buyer, or your best public relations representative, and what is worse—their well-being may be at risk.

Learn how to evaluate the student with "semi-objective criteria" and never hesitate to delay certification for the student who isn't ready. Then, do whatever is needed keep them in class and working toward becoming a diver. NEVER QUIT UNTIL THEY DO—AND NEVER LET THEM.

CHAPTER 5

Instructor Liability

To initiate a discussion about liability now is definitely *not* saving the best until last. It is a subject that is critical to all instructors and their students but, at the same time, is one of the things nobody wants to talk about.

Somehow, as I'm writing this I have this vision of plaintiff attorneys everywhere reading each word carefully to see if there is anything they can use against an instructor. If it's not an attorney, then for sure it's an expert witness for the plaintiff. So as long as I'm already feeling a little paranoid, I might as well address them directly and get it over with.

Neither this chapter, nor any other part of this book, is intended as a means of avoiding responsibility or liability of any kind. To the contrary, the very essence of the book is the acceptance of responsibility and the means to fulfill that responsibility in every sense of the word.

It should be made clear to the reader that I am not an attorney, and no effort is being made to offer legal advice or counsel. The information presented is simply my opinion based on my personal experience and observations over many years.

The practical matter of fact is that there is no defense against true negligence. If the instructor really is negligent, they will in all probability get nailed, and that may be only fair. On the other hand, it seems to me that the greatest majority of lawsuits stem not from instructor negligence, but from a plaintiff's desire to recapture medical costs, avoid their own responsibility and lay the blame on someone else. Or they (and/or possibly their attorney), see the situation as an opportunity to make some big bucks.

What this chapter is about is protecting yourself from legal problems based on someone's imagined omission in your course of instruction. I'm talking about things like a student having ear problems during an open water class and then later claiming the instructor didn't cover that in the course. Now, everyone in the class can vouch for the fact that it *was* covered, but if you can't actually prove that the victim was in attendance and had benefit of that information, you could be in trouble.

Naturally, there are many more serious things that can and do happen to people who participate in the sport of scuba diving. The primary purpose of this book is geared toward never letting a student go diving on their own until they are capable of doing so in a safe manner, and are fully qualified to participate without supervision. Unfortunately, virtually every human being seems to think they are bullet-proof until something goes wrong, and then they want to blame their failure on someone else.

There are lots of things an instructor needs to know about liability concerns, but they all seem to fall into three categories. They are:

- IF YOU TEACH SCUBA—YOU ARE AT RISK
- THERE ARE WAYS TO PROTECT YOURSELF
- HOW TO HANDLE AN ACCIDENT

Let's take a look at the various categories and see if we can make some sense of it all. Pay particular attention to the part on protecting yourself. It isn't about evading liability, but rather how to avoid frivolous lawsuits.

If You Teach Scuba— You Are at Risk

INSTRUCTOR LIABILITY

The instructor's liability exposure is not something you can define in a sentence or two, or even a couple of paragraphs. That's because responsibility varies from place to place, situation to situation, and you can be sure—it depends on how creative a plaintiff's attorney is.

There are a couple of things that need to be absolutely clear in the instructor's mind at the beginning of this little discourse. First, you must accept the fact that the student's well-being is in *your* hands. You are the person they trust and depend on to keep them safe. Second, you are bound by a standard-of-care within the area where you conduct classes, and third, all this has to be balanced with the minimum course standards set forth by the RSTC (Recreational Scuba Training Council) as well as the standards required by your certification agency.

All of the things mentioned above represent your greatest protection and your biggest exposure to liability. The standards and record keeping required by the certification agencies are designed to protect both you and the student and, if followed with reasonable common sense, can offer a high level of security for the student and act as your best defense in the event of an accident.

If an accident should happen, these same standards can also be your worst nightmare—especially if you have violated the written procedures of your certification agency or have been careless with your record keeping. Should that happen, the plaintiff's attorney will use every rule you violated against you, and every record you failed to keep will be used as evidence of your incompetence.

In addition, the specific do's and don'ts spelled out in the agency's training materials will also be used against you. For example, a student text tells the student that "a down line must always be used," but because of some special situation, a line isn't used on that particular class. If there is an accident, I'll almost guarantee you it will be used against you. So be very aware of what the agencies tell your students and be sure you "follow the book."

■ *STANDARD-OF-CARE* is a legal term used to describe the conduct of a fictitious, reasonable and prudent instructor. On a more practical level, it is what the student has a right to expect in a scuba course based on the course content taught by the majority of instructors within the area where the student intends to go diving, and best prepares the student to dive in the water conditions they are most likely to encounter.

For example, there is no need to teach drysuit usage in the tropics, but it may be considered standard equipment for use in frigid waters.

There are many examples of area-specific instruction, but the point is that if you teach somewhere that requires special consideration, the standard-of-care for that area demands that you provide the student with the instruction and information required to meet that standard-of-care—even if it isn't provided for in your certification agency's written standards. You must always remember that they are *minimum*—not maximum—standards, and should allow for the instructor to accommodate unusual conditions— providing the accommodations don't violate agency standards. While there are some agencies that won't like this approach and may even be opposed to it, it is my opinion that this is the best, and maybe the *only* way that new and better techniques can be developed.

INSTRUCTOR ERROR

This is one of those topics I just hate to write about. I would much rather there was no such thing as instructor error. But since that isn't real life, let me begin by saying that there doesn't need to be instructor error. At least there doesn't need to be the kind of error that is preventable with reasonable common sense.

There is no way to absolutely stop unforeseeable problems from developing—I suppose that's why they are called accidents. There are, however, ways to prevent the student from moving into harm's way.

■ *PREPARATION* is the biggest part of prevention. If the instructor makes sure that all systems are go before a class begins, the chances for problems are greatly reduced.

■ *SITE SELECTION* is important. Know the waters and be sure they are appropriate to the training being done, present no known safety concerns, and allow for student supervision by the instructor or their assistants.

■ **INSTRUCTOR REDAINESS** for the job at hand cannot be overstated. The instructor must be qualified and experienced for the class about to be taught.

■ **STUDENT READINESS** can be critical. Never knowingly allow a student to proceed to an open water class if they aren't qualified. And you mustn't push a student to do what they are reluctant to do. This isn't the military, it's a sport!

■ **SUPERVISION** of the student is very important. Clearly the student has an equal responsibility, since it would be physically impossible for the instructor to watch everyone all the time. Even so, you should only deal with as many students as it is practical to keep track of and respond to if the need arises. If standards or conditions dictate, use assistants. You may even want to go one-on-one to ensure the student's safety.

One of the greatest potential liability situations for the instructor is if you *purposely* lose sight of the student. Especially in the early part of the open water classes, before they are ready to move off on their own.

Ascent training is one place where the instructor may lose track if they send the student to the surface unescorted. Even if there is an assistant on the surface, if you lose visual contact with the student and they somehow get into trouble and don't reach the surface, you have a big problem.

■ **NEGLIGENCE** is very difficult to defend. Even unintentional negligence. Such things as prematurely leaving the students unsupervised, knowingly violating standards, or pushing the students beyond what is reasonable and prudent—leave the instructor in a very tentative position.

The best advice I can offer is to use good common sense and do everything you can reasonably be expected to do to keep the student from being put into a dangerous situation. Of course, no matter what you do as the instructor, there is no way to totally prepare for the student who does something stupid.

STUDENT ERROR

When the student makes a mistake, there is still the possibility that you may be blamed for it, even when the situation was beyond your control. The problem is, some attorney is going to say "you should have known," and the fact is, you may be legally responsible if the accident was foreseeable.

There are ways to protect yourself from this problem, but that comes later; first let's look at the kind of mistakes the student can make that may be construed as *your fault!*

■ *BAD JUDGMENT* on the part of the student can manifest itself in many ways. They can do everything from not telling you they are feeling bad to failing to follow your directions. Here is a short list of the kinds of mistakes students routinely make which sometimes end in disaster.

- *Failure to follow directions:* Even when you tell them exactly what to do, there will be those who either just don't get it, or are so set on their own agenda that they just don't care. If they go wandering off from the group, or perform the exercise improperly, or any of many things they shouldn't do—they put themselves and you at risk.

- *Failure to inform the instructor of problems or fears:* There is no way for you to see inside the head of the student and know what they are feeling. At least not for sure. There are signs that we covered earlier, but no way to really know.

    The student must tell you when they are afraid, too cold or tired, and especially when they don't feel well. You should be on guard for the tell-tale signs, but if they aren't readily apparent they are easy to miss. The problem is, if an accident occurs because the student failed to inform you, an attorney may still lay the blame at your door.

Your best protection is to give the student every opportunity to let you know of any problems, and state clearly that if they don't tell you a problem exists, you can't deal with it.

EQUIPMENT ERROR

Equipment error refers to the mistakes made while using the equipment, not to some error or problem with the equipment itself.

There is little point in rehashing all the mistakes that can be made with the equipment. We covered that pretty well in Chapter 2. On the other hand, it couldn't hurt just to remind ourselves of the kinds of mistakes that can be made with equipment.

■ *THE RIGHT EQUIPMENT* is fundamental. It must be appropriate to the kind of diving that the student will be doing. For example, a lycra skin in cold-water areas, or a rebreather for short, shallow dives would both be inappropriate. Make sure you teach with, and put your students into, equipment that is suited to the the kind of diving they intend to do.

■ *ENOUGH EQUIPMENT* is also important to the safety of the diver. For example, if they can't monitor the effects of time and pressure on their body they put themselves at great risk.

■ *PROPER MAINTENANCE* of equipment is key to proper function. You can't expect the equipment to perform at peak level if it is abused and not kept clean, well lubricated, and correctly adjusted at all times.

■ *CORRECT FIT AND ADJUSTMENT* are as important as all the rest. Remember, the equipment package should feel like it is part of your body, not a bunch of junk hanging on you. First make sure everything fits, and then adjust it all so it is in fact a unit.

These are just reminders about equipment usage. Refer back to Chapter 2 for details.

WHERE IT CAN HAPPEN

You might get the impression from my continued reference to open water classes that the open water is the only place you have any real liability. Not so! The moment a student or a diver comes under your care and custody, you have the potential for liability.

Responsibility really begins for the instructor the first time you tell them what to do and they attempt doing it. Sure, the likelihood of anything happening in the very early stages of a course is remote, but not impossible, so you should be on guard.

The first time there is any serious possibility of a problem is when the student enters the water. It doesn't matter whether it is in a pool or in confined open water, the stakes go up dramatically when they hit the water.

The instructor should be on the watch and carefully monitor each and every student to help them from getting into trouble. If need be, use qualified assistants to help keep track, although it is best if the instructor deals with only as many students as can be kept track of and responded to in an emergency.

The important thing to remember is that just because you are in a warm, clear pool, it doesn't mean that nothing can go wrong. It can, and it does!

THIRD PARTY INVOLVEMENT

The last major area of potential liability is to me the most worrisome. The reason it has always concerned me is that it involves a third party—an individual whose actions are unpredictable and beyond your control.

When a third party becomes involved, the most you can normally do is respond to a problem. It is virtually impossible to prevent whatever takes place due to the actions of the third party.

By now you're probably saying "what in the heck is he talking about?" Well, let me give you an example. The instructor sends a buddy team out on a compass run. One of the divers is having a problem getting under water, so the buddy decides to be helpful and pulls the struggling diver below the surface.

Being helped by your buddy to descend is fine if the diver is expecting to be pulled under. Let's suppose the diver was a little tired from the effort of trying to get beneath the surface and had just taken the regulator out of their mouth to rest a moment. Suddenly, and without warning, they find themselves being pulled under water in the middle of an exhalation. What happens? They may inhale some water and start choking, or they may be so surprised that they panic, in which case any of several things could happen. Whatever transpires, the results can be catastrophic. The problem is, since they were in class and under the instructor's care and custody, the finger of blame may be pointed at the instructor for "allowing" the student to be in that situation.

It would seem that any rational person would see that the situation I just described was completely beyond the instructor's control, but as I have pointed out numerous times throughout this chapter—a plaintiff attorney will do everything in their power to make the incident the instructor's fault.

■ **SUMMARY.** The only things you can do as an instructor are to teach according to the guidelines of your certification agency, and meet the standard of care for your area. In addition, you must be sure that the student is properly informed of both your responsibility to them, and their responsibility to you. Then you must attempt to anticipate—and be prepared at all times to respond to—any problems that might develop.

There is virtually nothing else that a reasonable person can expect of another human being.

I feel sure that by this time you must be half scared to death about all the potential liability. If so, I have accomplished what I set out to do. While I don't want to scare you to death, I do want to get your attention, and sometimes a person just has to see the worst possible scenario before they will pay attention to the ways to avoid putting themselves into a liability situation. This next section offers hope, but pay attention, because your professional future could depend on it.

Ways to Protect Yourself

Protecting yourself from liability should be pretty straight forward. All you should have to do is be conscientious and do your job right. If you do there won't be any problem. Right? Wrong! Way too many legal problems develop for instructors—not because they did something wrong—but because they didn't do everything they should have during the course that would have allowed them to *prove* they hadn't done anything wrong.

Before we jump into the how's and what's of protecting yourself from liability, I feel the need to clarify once more exactly what you are protecting yourself from. If you are *negligent* there is virtually no protection! The fact is, negligence means you messed up and will probably be held responsible. What you can protect yourself from is being wrongly accused of negligence when the problem was out of your control, or when some attorney wants to make it your fault based on some trumped-up omission in your teaching practices. Nothing here is intended as a means of evading responsibility, but as a means of avoiding frivolous accusations.

Much of what follows has already been covered to some extent. However, I want it documented in clear, concise terms. Protecting yourself, beyond doing a good job, boils down to two things: preparation and paperwork.

PREPARATION

Preparation covers a lot of territory. To be truly prepared there are five areas of consideration. Preparedness means you should:

- BE SURE THE STUDENT IS "READY"
- MAKE THE PROPER SITE SELECTION
- BE AWARE OF THE WATER CONDITIONS
- HAVE THE PROPER SAFETY EQUIPMENT
- HAVE EMERGENCY TRAINING

■ *BE SURE THE STUDENT IS "READY"* to do the dive. This means that they are prepared in every sense of the word. They must be ready mentally, physically, and in terms of their ability.

- Mentally, the student has to feel good about the dive and not be overly apprehensive. You want them to feel a *little* apprehensive so they are on their toes and paying attention, but if they are *afraid* and too reluctant, they should be given the chance to not participate. Ultimately they are the only ones who can make that decision.

- Physically, a student must be capable of performing the tasks asked of them. They don't need to be olympic athletes, but they must never knowingly put themselves at risk due to known physical limitations either. Here again, you can only observe the obvious; they are the ones who need to understand their own limitations and make the final decision on whether they are physically prepared to dive.
- Ability goes back to that subjective decision making process you must go through to determine if they are "ready." Remember, if you can answer *yes* to all the questions about their readiness, you have done all an instructor can do.

■ *MAKE THE PROPER SITE SELECTION,* one that is appropriate to the skill level of the students and fulfills the safety requirements. Choosing a dive site that meets the needs of the class includes reasonable access, the proper degree of difficulty, and suitable conditions.

- Access to the dive site is important because you don't want it to be too difficult for the student. Some sites are dangerous to get to and the student may be put at risk in the process.
- The degree of difficulty at the site refers to entry and exit as well as depth. A site that is too difficult to enter and exit will turn the student off and also puts them at unnecessary risk if it is beyond their comfort zone. The same is true for depth. You need enough depth to conduct the class, but not too much for their experience level.
- Conditions for diving generally refers to water conditions; however it can also mean weather and/or timing. Water conditions will be covered more thoroughly in the next section, but the timing of the dive and current weather conditions are important considerations as well. A dive planned too early or too late presents potential problems. Also, if the weather is bad it can have a negative effect on the students. Be sure you don't impose any unnecessary burden on the student by diving during bad conditions.

■ *BE AWARE OF THE WATER CONDITIONS* when you plan a dive and before you take students into the water. Not knowing exactly what you are getting into can be a serious mistake.

Ocean diving is much more changeable than freshwater diving. The tides, currents, and surf can have a profound effect on student safety as well as their enjoyment of the dive. The instructor needs to be aware of all the variables that affect conditions before putting the student in the water.

In the late '60s, I was teaching an instructor school in Rhode Island. The candidates were preparing to do their open water work, and I asked one of the candidates—who was a local diver—to place a marker buoy just off-shore. While I explained what we would be doing in the class, he went out to place the buoy. By the time the group entered the water, the tide had started out and when we got to where the buoy should have been—it was gone. The tide was so strong that the buoy had been forced under water by the current.

Naturally, the dive was aborted and everyone returned to shore. It was a great practical lesson about being prepared, but it could just as easily have been a disaster.

The point is, I should have known about—or at least checked on—the tides. As it was, I wasted half a day and very nearly put some divers into a dangerous situation. Since they were all instructor candidates who were very experienced divers, there was no problem. On the other hand, if they had been new students it could have been quite serious.

It isn't just tides and currents you need to be concerned about. Surf conditions can be just as dangerous, and temperature is also a big consideration. Being properly outfitted can help, but a diver who gets too cold can be in real trouble. Just like all other areas of risk, you shouldn't ever knowingly put the students in harm's way.

■ *HAVE THE PROPER SAFETY EQUIPMENT* on hand at all times. Basic equipment should include, but is not limited to, a first aid kit and oxygen delivery system. In addition, be sure you have access to emergency services and know their locations and telephone numbers.

If available, mobile communications is an excellent tool since it permits instant contact with emergency services, and can mean the difference in life and death to the victim of an accident.

■ *HAVE EMERGENCY TRAINING* in first aid and CPR because as the instructor, you will be the first responder in most cases. It isn't necessary to be an EMT, but you do need to know about the kinds of injuries that commonly occur in your local waters—like stings, cuts, etc.—and also be knowledgeable about the treatment of diving's more serious injuries, like embolism and other forms of barotrauma. Training in oxygen administration is a major plus for any instructor, and could mean the difference between life and death for an injured diver.

■ *SUMMARY.* Being prepared in the event of an accident is one part of the puzzle in learning how to protect yourself from unwarranted liability. The whole concept of being prepared is based on prevention. If you do all the things you should, the likelihood of an accident becomes pretty remote. Even so, in spite of your best efforts, every now and then someone gets hurt. If it happens to any of your students, being prepared to respond to the victim's needs can not only save their life, but may also protect you from responsibility.

The other part of protecting yourself has to do with paperwork. I know every instructor — maybe every human being — hates paperwork, but it is your very best line of defense against wrongful accusation of responsibility.

PAPERWORK

To everyone but the most detail oriented person, keeping records is the most unpleasant and bothersome part of scuba instruction. The truth is, the kind of personality that seeks out the adventure of scuba instruction is not the classic record keeping type. But if you are smart, no matter how much you dislike keeping those records, you will learn to do it in every detail. If you don't, and you are sued, you will find out very quickly that a little bit of time spent during the class may very likely have been the difference in whether or not someone attempts to hold you accountable.

There are three areas of record keeping that are critical. They are:

- FULL DISCLOSURE TO THE STUDENT
- RECORD KEEPING FOR THE INSTRUCTOR/STORE
- THE STUDENT'S LOG SYSTEM

■ *FULL DISCLOSURE TO THE STUDENT* has two purposes. The first, and most important, is the safety of the student. They need to know *exactly* what they are getting into so they can decide *not* to do it if they feel it is beyond their ability.

The second purpose is for your protection. In order for a release of liability to be fully effective, the student must be able to give *informed consent*. That means that they have been fully informed about everything and, knowing the potential dangers, release you from anything that might go wrong during the instruction process.

There are lots of ways to inform the students about course content. You should always explain verbally what is in store for them, but if legal problems develop you may have to rely on the other students' memory—and you can trust me on this one—they won't remember what you want them to. No, you really need another, better way to prove you fully informed each and every one of them, so there is no question they knew what they were getting into.

The most effective way to inform your students is with a standardized visual presentation. Risk Awareness videos are available that not only tell the student what they will be doing, but show them where and how it will be done. The videos are quite thorough and cover what is involved in scuba instruction. They should be shown prior to beginning the course and again before open water classes.

A Statement of Understanding that clearly explains both the instructor's *and* the student's responsibilities is also very important since it restates what you told them as well as what they saw and heard on the video, if one was used.

One other thing that is essential to the process of informing the students is written confirmation of the fact that they saw, heard, and read everything *before* they signed the release. The confirmation must be signed by the students and placed in their permanent file so that they can't claim at some future time they didn't see, hear, or read the information.

All the certification agencies have access to the written and visual support you need to protect yourself from unwarranted accusation. Rely on them to provide the means, but only you can provide the follow-through. The tools work only if you use them.

■ *RECORD KEEPING FOR THE INSTRUCTOR/STORE* is the second part of protecting yourself from unfounded legal assault.

I've already said that the student must be fully informed *before* they sign a release of liability, but there is more to it than that. Records must be kept for everything the student does and everything they are told during the entire course. Not only that, but timing is also critical. They must sign off *after* they have been informed, and *before* they do the next skill. Let's take a little closer look at the kinds of records that need to be kept. They include releases, medicals, and verification of all procedures.

- Releases are a very important part of the record-keeping process. They are the one place where the student has agreed in legal terms that they understand that sometimes things happen which are beyond the control of the instructor. And if that should happen, or the students themselves do something stupid, they or their survivors won't hold the instructor responsible. Now I hope you realize that this is a gross simplification of releases, and that you need to learn more specifics from your certification agency. However, it does present the essence of the intent.

- Medicals are another important part of your protection because they tell you up front if your student has any physical problems you should be aware of that might preclude them from taking the class at all. The medical also keeps you from having to attempt to make any judgments about the students that you aren't qualified to make.

  The student's medical record should be a permanent part of their file. You never know when it may be necessary for you to prove that there was no medical reason given to you at the time of the course to prevent the student from attending classes, and if there was a problem that existed, you weren't informed of it.

- Verification of all procedures is the last part of protecting yourself. It is also the part that instructors find most bothersome. I think the reason it is so problematic for the instructor is because it is such a repetitive thing to do. Having *every* student acknowledge *every* action at *every* step can be more than a little tedious.

While keeping detailed records is annoying, it is the single most important protection you have against future legal challenges. In the first place, it shows you are conscientious about details—all details. It also verifies the student's participation in the classwork, and their agreement with you that they completed each step of the course satisfactorily and were ready to proceed to the next part. The latter makes it difficult for them to claim later they didn't do or didn't know something.

There are some important timing considerations in record keeping that were mentioned earlier. It is very important that all verifications be completed *after* the exercise has been done, and *before* they move to the next one. This might seem obvious and you might even wonder why I mention it again. Well, instructors have the bad habit of letting students sign-off in bunches. That is, they have them sign for several exercises at once—after the fact.

Signing off later would be fine if nothing ever went wrong, but since the whole idea is to protect yourself in case something does go wrong, the timing becomes critical. You can see that signing in bunches is just perfunctory and is subject to being discredited at a later date. Never ask the student to verify completion of an activity *before* the fact.

The final part of the paperwork puzzle has to do with the student's own record—their log book. This record can be just as important to the instructor as their own records. Let's look at why.

■ *THE STUDENT'S LOG SYSTEM* is part and parcel of the record keeping process. It is as important to the instructor as it is to the student, but for different reasons.

For the student, the log is a permanent record of their own, covering every aspect of their diving life. It documents all of their formal training, every level of certification and type of training they have completed, and all of their diving experiences.

For the instructor, the student's record of their activities, especially when combined with the records of other class members, can become a powerful statement about the instructor's conduct and attitude toward the class. Of course if the conduct was poor, it becomes an equally *bad* statement of the instructor's ability.

Problems can develop for the student if their original instructor gives up teaching, or perhaps the facility where they first became certified goes out of business. If this should happen, the student's log becomes the primary record of their diving history. It may in fact be the only way to prove they have completed a course, or perhaps even several courses. In addition, many of the diving operations around the world are more concerned with the diver's actual experience than with what cards they carry. This means that the log book—at least in some areas—becomes more important than a certification card.

■ *THE INSTRUCTOR'S LOG* is also important. Like the student, there may be times when it is the only available record of the proceedings of a particular class.

It is quite common for student records to be kept by the retail scuba store instead of the instructor. Generally this makes sense, but on occasion a store goes out of business and the instructor loses contact with the records. If this should happen, the instructor's log may become the principal source of information.

The instructor's log is also a permanent record of their own education and experience. This record is valuable in many different ways for future educational efforts and recognition of the instructor's experience. It can be so important that it would be difficult to identify every conceivable use of the instructor's log.

It should be sufficient here to simply say that every instructor, in this day and age, should keep a detailed log of their diving life— including all class proceedings.

The last part of protecting yourself has to do with what goes on if an accident does occur. There is an overwhelming emotional side to an accident that frequently brings out the fool in all of us. Right after the accident occurs is when clear, calm thinking is essential. Let's look at some things you should and shouldn't do in the event of an accident.

HOW TO HANDLE AN ACCIDENT

When an accident happens, there is a great deal of confusion. The instructor is trying to care for the victim, there are bystanders and other students milling around — all trying to offer advice and beginning to make judgments about what happened. In the throws of all that confusion, a lot of mistakes can be made by everyone at hand, especially in determining what actually did take place.

During the first minutes after the victim has been dealt with, the people standing around speculating are likely to try and make some sense of what happened and attempt to come up with their own idea of what transpired. When a witness attempts to recall later just what they saw, they will be confused to some extent by the conflict between what they really saw and what they talked about with others right after the accident. What is more, given time to reflect, their personal feelings about the participants will begin to creep into their memory and affect their recollection of the events.

For these and other good reasons, the instructor must be prepared with a course of action to be followed as soon as the victim is under medical care. This is the time when all involved will have the clearest idea of what took place and will be the least inclined to make judgments. The suggested procedure is to:

- REMAIN CALM
- IDENTIFY ALL WITNESSES
- SECURE VICTIM'S EQUIPMENT
- NOTIFY VICTIM'S FAMILY
- WRITE DOWN YOUR OWN ACCOUNT
- NOTIFY YOUR CERTIFICATION AGENCY/
  INSURANCE CONTACT

■ *REMAIN CALM* at all costs. Your actions will, to a large extent, affect the other people and determine to some degree how they feel about you later.

The instructor should never speculate on how or why the injury happened. In the first flush of the moment the instructor may feel guilt for something that was totally out of their control. It will serve no good purpose to start guessing about what happened.

The exception to that might be with law enforcement people. You should cooperate based on *what you know for sure*, but not speculate about what *might* have been.

■ *IDENTIFY ALL WITNESSES* and get their names and contact information as soon as possible. People have a tendency to drift away quickly and not want to get involved, so the sooner you identify them the better.

I have been advised by attorneys that while you shouldn't discuss the accident with the students—since it may taint their view of what happened—it is perfectly fine and quite important to get them to write down exactly what they saw happen. Don't ask them to make judgments, but simply recount what they believed transpired. Collect all this from the various witnesses and turn it all over to your legal representative.

It is almost standard procedure now for the insurance company to send an investigator out immediately after a serious accident, to do in-depth interviews with the witnesses to verify their recollection of what happened. This is to your benefit and they should get all of your cooperation.

■ *SECURE THE VICTIM'S EQUIPMENT* and either turn it over to the proper authority, or secure it so it can't be tampered with. It is really in your best interest to give it to a responsible third party so there can be no question about how the equipment was cared for. If possible, you should be present when the equipment is tested.

■ *NOTIFY THE VICTIM'S FAMILY* as soon as possible. Be kind and considerate, and help them any way you can. Do not discuss the accident or speculate on what happened or who was responsible. They may want to blame someone at some point, or at least find out exactly what happened. But initially they need your comfort and consideration. Being kind and considerate may also help reduce their desire to blame you later.

■ *WRITE DOWN YOUR OWN ACCOUNT* of what transpired. This is more important than I can tell you. If you are sued at a later time, you are unlikely to remember all the details. If you document everything you can remember with times, dates, names, places, and even comments made that you might have overheard—you will have a very powerful defense weapon should you need it.

Do not give this account to anyone other than your attorney. Good or bad, it *will* be used against you in the wrong hands.

■ *NOTIFY YOUR CERTIFICATION AGENCY/INSURANCE CARRIER* at the earliest opportunity. Not only are you required to do so, but they are your support system for such occurrences.

They will want an accident report on what happened, and will advise you as to how to proceed. Follow their directions without exception. They have dealt with these problems before and know the best way to handle them.

You must remember that even though the victim or their survivor may express that they don't hold you responsible at the time, once an attorney gets in touch with them, they may change their minds. That is why it is so important to get as much detail from witnesses and yourself as possible. Also, if the victim survives, get them to make a statement as well.

I'm quite sure that the direct nature of what I have been saying sounds like legal advice. Let me assure you that it isn't. Most of the procedure has been suggested by insurance carriers and reviewed by several attorneys. In addition, years of experience with instructors who have had accidents—and made all the mistakes I have warned you about—have taught me the simple realities of what happens when your worst nightmare comes true.

■ *SUMMARY.* Every instructor knows that there is always the possibility of an accident lurking out there somewhere. It is a part of the profession that is a reality, but a part that nobody wants to think about. It is simply unacceptable to believe that it could ever happen to you. In fact, I believe that if any instructor actually thought that they might be involved in an accident at some time—they probably wouldn't teach.

There are some instructors who mistakenly believe that because they have insurance they don't need to worry about it, and therefore just put the possibility out of their mind. The reality is that life is a risk. Everyday, everything we do carries a certain amount of risk with it. Driving to work or walking across the street all too often can result in an accident—even death.

It would be naive, even foolhardy, to think for a moment that entering an environment where a human cannot sustain life without the support of man-made equipment is anything less than a significant risk.

The society we live in today seems absolutely unwilling to accept any kind of personal responsibility for their own actions. Even when they knowingly place themselves in harm's way, they want someone else to be responsible when something goes wrong. At times, it appears that even the legal system—or maybe *especially* the legal system—contributes to people's need to either blame others for their personal shortcomings or grab the opportunity to actually profit from them monetarily.

Gone are the days when we "paid our money and took our chances." The legal atmosphere simply no longer allows us to be cavalier in our approach to how we deal with other people. This is especially true in high risk adventure sports such as scuba diving.

Today's scuba instructor is obliged to follow carefully designed programs of instruction, adhere to strict standards, and be able to rely on detailed records in order to meet the standard-of-care in scuba instruction. This is a formidable task for individuals who may not by nature be detail oriented.

Most divers become instructors because they love the sport and want to help share it with others. They are adventurous, fun loving people who initially see the excitement and pleasure of teaching, but may not be quite prepared for the rigors of the details.

Well, don't despair! It isn't all that bleak. In fact, the certification agencies are constantly working to make the instructor's job easier and less threatening. There are many ways to protect the student and yourself from danger, and just being diligent in how you teach and the records you keep can provide great peace of mind.

Liability for your actions, like risk in all parts of our lives, is just the natural order of things. If you want others to be responsible for their actions, you must be prepared to be responsible for your own.

If you find yourself involved in an accident, and you follow the prescribed procedures and accurately record the process—you are about as safe from unwarranted liability as life is likely to allow.

C H A P T E R   6

Afterthoughts

If you made it this far in the book you may be feeling like that bumper sticker you see on the back of trucks that says "If you can read this, you're too close." I say that because you had to wade through chapter one about why people learn and why they don't in order to get to the more interesting stuff. Now that you've read it, you might very well be asking yourself why you were interested in becoming a diving instructor in the first place.

It would be pretty easy to get the impression from this book that there are lots of potential problems with teaching people to dive. That's because there are. At the same time though, there is a positive side to the process that I may not have made abundantly clear. In addition, there are a few little odds and ends about the complete process that I would like to expound on. So just to round out my views of what diving instruction is all about, let's examine some afterthoughts.

The Joy of Teaching Scuba

We certainly have covered most, if not all, of the potential pitfalls of teaching scuba. It seems to me that it was necessary to do so in order to get your attention. And also to give you a deeper sense of the seriousness of what you are undertaking so you might fully appreciate the magnitude of the job.

What I don't want to do is leave the impression that teaching diving is all problems. On the contrary, as I said in the beginning, teaching people to dive is one of the most rewarding and pleasurable things you will ever do. It's just that understanding the problems is what makes it possible to enjoy the process.

To be able to take an individual who seemingly lacks the aptitude, and mold them into a safe, confident diver is a huge thrill. But the entire process of opening up the student's mind, and filling it with usable information that expands their life in some meaningful way, is one of the most satisfying things any person can hope for.

For the best instructors, teaching diving is more than a vocation or even an avocation. It is a way of life. It permeates everything you do. It is your job, your recreation, your social life, and the way you fulfill your need to be productive.

There are two ways to look at students. One way, which unfortunately seems to be the most common, is to view them as customers passing through the classes simply to provide the instructor with an income. Students get very little from courses taught by this type of instructor, beyond the mechanical introduction to diving, and they leave with only a fraction of what it's really all about.

The instructor that chooses the other path is the one this book was written for. Those of you who grasp the essence of what this book is about will recognize that there is much more to it than collecting the course fee and showing up for class. My kind of instructor takes on the whole package.

The Holistic Approach
to Scuba Instruction

The process of teaching scuba is like a giant circle of events, each of which interrelates with all of the other parts that make up the circle. It can be thought of as a symbiotic relationship between all segments of the diving industry. Just as the clown fish is permitted to live safely within the arms of the poisonous sea anemone so they might help each other to gather food, so do all the various parts of the scuba industry depend on each other to support the diver and themselves. Let's take a brief look at the parts that make up the circle and how they interlock.

THE STUDENT

It all begins with the student because they require the most support from all sources. You need to accept the fact that students, even once they become certified divers, are very high maintenance.

First the student must learn to dive. For this they need the instructor and everything it takes to support the process. Their training materials come from the certification agencies who initially trained the instructor and ultimately provide proof of the student's training. The retail store provides the facilities, the source of students, the equipment—and in many cases they also provide ongoing social activities and travel programs. In addition, they supply air fills for the tanks, service for the equipment, and continuing education for those who want more than an introduction to diving.

The manufacturer builds their equipment, the resorts provide the opportunity, and the charter services provide the means. Last but not least are the travel people who organize the trips for the retailers and provide customers for the resorts and charter services.

SALES

For some reason, to a lot of people selling is a euphemism for "trick the people out of their hard earned money." For this and other reasons, it seems that many instructors tend to think of teaching as "pure" and "selling" as evil and tainted. They love to teach, but don't want anything to do with selling. Yuck!

Within the context of scuba diving, since it is impossible to go diving without equipment, selling should mean "helping the student into the best equipment they can afford so they can enjoy the sport safely."

It is virtually impossible to separate instruction and sales. Especially since every diver must have the equipment and there is no one they trust more than the instructor.

The instructor is in a very unique position. They really don't ever need to sell in the traditional sense of the word. They don't have to convince a student they need equipment. They don't need to convince them to be a customer, and they don't have to sell themselves as a reliable authority on the subject. All this is done. The need and the motivation to buy are already there. The instructor has the enviable job of simply helping the student sort out what they can afford and want to buy.

This whole process is an integral part of the holistic circle. When you fill the student's need for equipment, you make a profit for the retailer, who provides you a job. The manufacturer makes money, which allows research and development of new, better, and easier-to-use equipment. You also provide customers for travel, resorts, and charter operations. Each of these use their profits to provide additional jobs and better facilities for everyone.

RETAILERS

Next to the student, the retailer is the most integral part of the circle. They bring together all aspects of the industry under one roof. They recruit the student, employ the instructor, supply the equipment and services, sell the travel, and provide the social fulfillment once the student is certified.

Without the retailer, there would be no industry. They are the source for virtually everything the diver needs.

Without the retailer there would be no outlet for equipment, and no customers for travel or charters. For a while there would be a few discount stores and mail-order houses, but without the supply of new divers produced by the retailers there would soon be no customers for either of these.

On the other hand, without the certification agencies, the manufacturers, the resorts, and the travel people there would be no way for the retailer to operate. No way to teach, nothing to sell, and nothing to do with it if there was. As you can see, everything begins and eventually ends with the students and the retailer. All other components of the industry work in concert to support and supply these two entities.

THE MANUFACTURER

Unless the instructors teach and sell the equipment available from the retailer, there is no need for the manufacturer. Like every product, they are only as viable as their customer base.

It is essential to the ongoing health of each manufacturer that the instructor, the retailer and their employees do their part in creating safe divers who must have the equipment to go diving.

TRAVEL AND RESORTS

The travel and resort operations would like to view themselves as not dependent on the circle. Many resorts are the first contact a customer has with diving, and since the resort can also teach classes and sell equipment, there is some tendency to believe they can stand alone.

The truth is, the resorts need the instructors to teach, the retailers to provide an ongoing customer base of certified divers, and the manufacturers to supply equipment. Since the resorts could never sell enough equipment to justify manufacturing, or train enough divers to sustain a certification agency, they too are an integral part of the holistic process.

The travel groups are subject to the same limitations as the resorts, so they are also deeply dependent on the symbiotic relationship of all segments of the diving industry.

THE MEDIA

Up to now I have failed to include the role of the media in the circle. They are also part of the holistic process.

The media is how the various segments communicate with each other, and especially with the divers. They inform the diver of what new equipment is available, the latest education, the most exotic diving locations, the trips to take them there, and in addition they keep us all aware of outside influences on our sport. As you can see, the media is a very important part of the industry and as such can have a very profound effect on its success or failure.

Without whipping this horse any longer, I think it should be abundantly clear that we are all part of a bigger picture. No one of the players are more important to the process than any other. Some, like the students and the retailers, are a little higher maintenance, but even they are just parts of the greater whole.

The next time a student asks you about equipment, or the retailer urges you to be more of a salesperson, remember that without the sales you will eventually be out of a job. Not just because the retailer won't make a profit, but more importantly, because the people you are teaching are unable to participate in the sport without the equipment.

The Instructor as an Employee

While some of you who become instructors will wind up being the employer, most will be the employee. As such there are some cold hard facts of life that you should understand. In fact, I believe that if you really do understand what I'm about to say, not only will you be a better employee, but you will also be a better employer.

THE COLD HARD FACTS

If the conduct of business was just numbers—which thankfully it isn't—the employees would be considered in the same cold light as any product on the showroom floor. That is, the employee's production would be measured just like a product's.

A good business person allots a certain amount of space and investment to a product. To be successful, that product must deliver a return on investment relative to the amount of space it is allotted or that space will either be diminished or removed altogether. That's only good business. If a product doesn't sell, get rid of it and replace it with one that does.

In many respects, an employee faces the same standard for production that the product does. The owner hires someone to help them increase their business, either in sales or in support of sales. If the employee fails to either increase the sales or provide valuable support that allows others to increase sales, they are simply wasting the owner's valuable resources. When this happens, common sense says that the employee must be replaced by someone who can produce what the business needs.

Naturally all this is tempered by numerous variables that make up a relationship between an employee and the employer. However, the underlying truth remains — either you produce or you are expendable. It's nothing personal, it's just the way life is.

As an employee, you must recognize this basic economic reality and realize that just because you crawl out of bed and show up for work on time—doesn't mean that you are fulfilling your obligation to either your employer or to yourself.

No one owes you anything in life. In fact, you are extremely fortunate when someone gives you the chance to get ahead. When it happens, you are the *only one* who can decide whether or not to take advantage of the opportunity. The best way to make a lot of money for yourself is to make a lot of money for your company.

Having said that, it should be noted that the employer has an equal responsibility to provide the employee with the training and the tools required in order to be successful. But assuming that kind of environment exists, then the responsibility for succeeding rests solely with the employee.

Putting it All Together

I hope you can see now that there's a lot more to being a quality instructor than just going to an instructor school and getting a certification. It takes a caring nature and lots of hands-on experience to develop the skill to mold an individual into a diver. While you may come equipped with the caring nature, gaining the experience takes some time.

All through history, before formal education was available, people learned their craft through the apprentice system. A young person who showed an aptitude for a craft was taken under the wing of a master. Over time they gradually learned the skills until one day they became a master themselves.

Once people recognized that the apprentice system could be accelerated with a concentrated course of study, formal education was born. While education can certainly provide the student with the information and even the tools needed to do a job, it still requires hands-on experience to learn the hard lessons required to become a master.

You would be well advised to take this same approach to becoming a scuba instructor. The instructor school will show you how the teaching system works, and how classes are taught. It will even give you many guidelines on how to get the job done. But it will require working with a great many students before you develop the frame of reference that only time and experience can give you. Don't rush it! Take your time and work with more experienced instructors until you begin to develop the feeling that you've been there before, and that you know the answer to the students' problems and can truly help them.

The Final Word

Do your best at all times to help people be successful—and never put unwarranted barriers in their way. Be considerate about the safety and comfort of the student at all times. Help them into the best equipment they can afford since they can't go diving without it. Do whatever it takes to get the job done correctly—and NEVER LET 'EM QUIT!

ABOUT THE AUTHOR

Bob Clark is truly one of the "old timers" in the diving business. He's been teaching people to be scuba instructors since 1965—and was teaching them to be divers before that.

In the early part of Bob's career he was a course director for YMCA—then in 1967 he helped design the NASDS instructional course and was Director of Education for that program until 1970, when he co-founded Scuba Schools International. As a founder of SSI he was also their principle instructor trainer until 1974, at which time more staff was added which allowed Bob to spend most of his time as President and CEO— although he was never very far from the training of the instructors.

Over the years Bob has either written or co-written a huge body of materials for training both scuba divers and scuba instructors. His most recognized efforts include the original Jeppesen diver training materials—which were co-written with John Lawson and Jon Hardy— and the SSI Instructor training program. A very great deal of what Bob developed for these programs has become part and parcel of what are now standard training practices around the world.

This book represents the essence of Bob's attitudes about being an instructor and how students should be trained. Even more, it speaks to what are the student's responsibilities, the instructor's responsibilities, and how both deserve to be treated. Reading this book can't help but give you a whole new outlook on how you deal with your students from now on.

Bob has retired from active teaching, but remains very involved in the development of cutting edge materials. If anything, the years have made him more intent on finding the best, most effective methods for training safe, confident divers.

Bob currently lives in Fort Collins, Colorado with his wife and life-long companion Marilyn—close to their children, grandchildren and his beloved mountains. He also spends several months each year in Arizona, where he trades his diving gear in for golf clubs and enjoys the warm desert winters.